10/14

‖‖‖‖‖‖‖‖‖‖‖‖‖‖‖‖‖‖‖‖
D0678100

THE DEAD ARE WATCHING

Photo By Rod L. Short

About the Author

Debra Robinson is a professional psychic and carries on a dual career in music as a performer and songwriter.

She works with Haunted Heartland Tours (www .hauntedhistory.net) and as a floating member of several paranormal investigation groups. Debra does private readings and volunteers for various online metaphysical sites. She heads JSMS, an annual charity skating event, and lives in a haunted house in a small town in Ohio.

For more information, visit www.DebraRobinson.net.

DEBRA ROBINSON

THE DEAD
ARE
WATCHING

GHOST STORIES FROM A RELUCTANT PSYCHIC

Llewellyn Publications
Woodbury, Minnesota

FIRST EDITION
First Printing, 2014

Book design by Bob Gaul
Cover design by Kevin R. Brown
Cover image: iStockphoto.com/20950719/©Ivan Bliznetsov
Editing by Ed Day

Llewellyn Publications is a registered trademark of Llewellyn Worldwide Ltd.

Library of Congress Cataloging-in-Publication Data
Robinson, Debra, 1955–
  The dead are watching: ghost stories from a reluctant psychic/Debra Robinson.
—First Edition.
    pages cm
  ISBN 978-0-7387-4046-1
1. Ghosts. I. Title.
  BF1461.R615 2014
  133.1—dc23
                              2014004788

Llewellyn Publications does not participate in, endorse, or have any authority or responsibility concerning private business transactions between our authors and the public.

All mail addressed to the author is forwarded, but the publisher cannot, unless specifically instructed by the author, give out an address or phone number.

Any Internet references contained in this work are current at publication time, but the publisher cannot guarantee that a specific location will continue to be maintained. Please refer to the publisher's website for links to authors' websites and other sources. Cover model(s) used for illustrative purposes only and may not endorse or represent the book's subject.

Llewellyn Publications
A Division of Llewellyn Worldwide Ltd.
2143 Wooddale Drive
Woodbury, MN 55125-2989
www.llewellyn.com

Printed in the United States of America

Contents

Part Two: Returns from Beyond

Acknowledgments

I'd like to thank all the friends and acquaintances who provided their stories for this book. Many of you opened your hearts to tell sad tales of loved ones who had passed away and then returned to say goodbye. I personally know how that feels. Special thanks to Michele and Tammy for their daily cheerleading; to Sandy for all the encouragement; to Brian and Lena, Sherri Brake, and Darrin and Danielle for their expertise and stories; to my editor Amy for all her guidance; and to Llewellyn Worldwide. This book is dedicated to my family and to Joyce Veece, James, Deebs, and last but certainly not least, God—with much thanks, for giving me "hope and a future."

Introduction

In my last book, I laid my soul bare, wondering if embracing the paranormal world may have influenced the tragic outcomes of my father and son. I think I made a good case for myself and, if nothing else, hopefully I helped a few readers choose their paths a bit more carefully. That's my greatest wish. But as in all true stories, as life unfolds, more happens. Our understanding changes and deepens, and mysteries unravel, leading to a core truth. I believe we must always work to find the truth, even though it may be buried deeply in the heart of a mystery wrapped in an enigma. For me, this truly describes ghosts, spirits, and the afterlife.

I was born into a psychic though religious family. Many of the females in the maternal line, including both my mother and her mother, were psychic. My grandmother descended from Alice Nutter, one of the infamous Lancashire Witches executed by King James in 1612.

But I'd fought against the very idea of these psychic abilities for most of my life, unable to reconcile them with my religious upbringing. Out of necessity, I finally began to embrace my psychic abilities. Shortly after doing so, my only child, my son James, was tragically killed at age twenty-four by a drunk driver, followed closely after by my father's suicide. This seemed more than just a coincidence. Then my son's returns from the other side began, and forced me on a difficult journey of despair, self-blame, and, ultimately, acceptance. My father returned only once—to snap his fingers in our faces the night we found his body. James still returns. But the premonitions James had of his own death and the actual events leading up to it were far stranger than mere coincidence. This true story was all recounted in my first book, a psychic memoir titled *A Haunted Life: The True Ghost Story of a Reluctant Psychic.* In my darker moments, when I missed Dad and James the most, my hard-won acceptance wavered. I still had doubts; I still had questions. I knew I still didn't have all the answers. And I knew I had to dig deeper, for my own peace of mind.

This is a book about my ongoing experiences with hauntings, whether they involved the return of a loved one after their death or a spirit I ran across during a paranormal investigation. I gathered the stories from investigators, friends and family, even a few strangers. You'd be surprised at how many people these things happen to. Or maybe you wouldn't be—I have a feeling anyone who picks up this book already knows that ghosts are real, that death isn't the end, and that strange stories of similar instances abound.

I grew up in a family who knew these things happen from personal experience. There were always spooky tales being told. Many may have sounded too crazy to be true, but they were told as gospel to us kids. I remember one family story that used to freak out my cousin Joyce. Our great-grandmother's brother earned the nickname Peg-leg after he lost his lower limb in an accident. Right after it happened, he suffered from what are now known as phantom limb pains. That's what the condition is called when you lose an arm or leg, but your brain hasn't quite caught up with the information and thinks it's still there. Sufferers swear they can still feel the limb attached, just as it always was. Often, the phantom limb is causing them some kind of pain or itching, that sort of thing.

In Peg-leg's case, he swore the toes on the missing leg were crossed. He begged anyone who came by his house to help him. The "leg" was excruciatingly painful for him.

Peg-leg's relatives had buried the appendage in the cemetery in a burial plot that had long been reserved for the old man. Finally, Peg-leg talked one of his family members into digging up his amputated leg and checking the toes. The relative went on this macabre mission to the cemetery, spooked by the task. And sure enough, when he dug the leg up, the toes were crossed. The relative uncrossed them and reburied the leg.

Yesterday upon the stair, I met a leg that wasn't there. Of course, I'm being silly here, paraphrasing the old Antigonish poem, but this is what we grew up with in my family—haunted houses, psychic abilities, weird stories, and just the right mindset on a dark night to make it all even creepier. You may have grown up with the same thing. If not, welcome to my world! Settle back, turn on all the lights, and read this book. Whether you are a believer or not, the true stories contained within will make you think. And if you are a skeptic, they may just change your mind.

PART ONE
INVESTIGATIONS AND EVIDENCE

All of us in the paranormal world have stories. Something happened to almost each and every one of us who hunt for ghosts, use psychic abilities, or chase after the holy grail of evidence. We each came to our beliefs in some personal way, and it usually involved contact with the other side whether we wanted it or not. Eventually, most of us began to search in earnest. We bought the equipment to capture the unseen voices or photograph forms invisible to the naked eye. We honed our psychic abilities or our technological expertise, and we went in search of hauntings. Most of us found them.

1

THE WITCH

The stench in the room was tangible, like a living thing that clung to the throat, filling my nostrils and lungs, choking me. A thin shaft of moonlight snuck through a slit in the huge blocks high on the wall, illuminating a small dry spot on the cold stone floor. I stepped gingerly, barefoot, toward the pool of light, carefully avoiding the puddles of urine and piles of human excrement completely covering its surface, except for this one small spot. Needing to relieve myself badly, gagging, then stumbling and sliding in the filth, I was desperate to reach the only clean place to do so.

"Please," I whispered desperately. "Please, please."

The sound of my own voice whimpering woke me from the depressing dream. I was sick to my stomach with misery, and despair filled my soul. I'd had this dream at least twenty times throughout my life, ever since I was a teenager. It always left me with a sense of desolation that took days to shake off. One look at the clock told me that I hadn't had near enough sleep, and it was doubtful that I would now. I sighed as I thought about the plans I'd made to help a family in a haunted house that afternoon.

As I showered and went about my routine, I thought about the dream. At first, when I began to have the dream as a young woman, all I knew was that it felt real and that *I* was the woman trying to find the clean spot on the floor to go to the bathroom. Later, when I learned about my ancestress Alice Nutter, I put two and two together and began to wonder. Through some strange memory, or maybe even a past life, could I be experiencing Alice being chained to the floor of that dungeon with her fellow witches waiting to be hanged? Over the years, the dream was always the same; sometimes I got more of a glimpse of the surroundings and other times I got more of the feelings associated with it. Recently, through the help of modern technology—the internet—I'd seen inside Lancaster Castle, where Alice was taken. I stared at the dungeon steps leading to the darkness below and scrutinized the iron rings the prisoners were bolted to. After seeing it, I felt as if this was the place I'd always dreamed about.

I dried my hair, shaking off the memories of the recent past, *and* perhaps the distant past as well, and focused on the upcoming investigation. *For a believer in signs and omens, this is not a good way to start the day.*

———

I didn't really want to go on this investigation. I hoped and prayed it would be canceled, as it had been twice before. Something about it just didn't sit right with me, and it made me nervous. This did happen sometimes. The thought of facing the unknown—hauntings, spirits, even possibly the demonic—left me uneasy. Even after a lifetime of dealing with the paranormal, it was anything but routine. But the investigation wasn't canceled, and it was pouring rain as well when our team of paranormal investigators gathered at the small one-and-a-half-story, brick house on the outskirts of a town forty minutes north of where I live.

One by one we pulled our cars into the driveway, sheets of rain drumming on the roofs, the force of it splashing at the muddy puddles. Though my unease had started with the dream that day, it continued with the sensation apparently emanating from the large house on the hill to my right. I sat behind the wheel for a moment, glancing up at it. It loomed over the small house we were investigating that evening.

Just to the right of that big house sat a squat, brown hodgepodge-looking building that resembled someone's *idea* of a house. It had jutting additions that screamed afterthought and a general air of neglect. This smaller house had that bad feeling emanating from it as well. I stepped out of the car and stood there in the mud staring, with the rain running down my hood and into my eyes. The sudden slamming of the other car doors snapped me back to the present, and I followed the team into the small house that was supposed to be haunted.

As soon as I walked in, I could feel it strongly: something was here. After meeting the family, my investigator friend Brian, who was also the founder of the Massillon Ghost Hunters Society, asked me to go back outside.

"Debra, we're going to walk through with the family to hear about the haunting and the hotspots," he told me. "Can you please wait in the car until we do?" This is what usually happens with a psychic on an investigation. To be beyond reproach, a psychic shouldn't have any preconceived notions about a house. I agree with this and never want to know anything in advance. This leaves me as close to a psychically clean slate as possible, open only to what comes in clairvoyantly.

Back outside in the car, I sat staring through the windshield and the still-pouring rain as I waited. I was focused on the house on the hill. *Watching, I'm watching, I hide, but I'm watching*, said the voice inside my head. A cold chill ran through me, and my left side tingled, which is how I've always known when psychic information is coming in. But I couldn't make any sense of it.

Something else was here, continued the voice in my head, the layers of history all swirling and mashing together, confusing me and making my mind dart about for answers. The entire area of ground on both sides of this little house just felt bad. I could sense fear—old fear and chaos to the left of the little house, and newer fear to the right of it, toward the big house on the hill.

My friend Brian soon leaned out the back door into the driving rain and beckoned me inside. After briefly explaining the group's methods to the family, Brian led the way as the family settled in to wait quietly downstairs. We each announced our names for the digital recorders, and the four of us, the investigation team members that night, started up the creaky stairs.

A small room with a center stairwell and slanted ceilings stretched out before me as Brian intoned the standard introductions used for taped sessions. The upstairs was bare of furniture, with just some boxes and an old bed mattress propped against one wall. While Brian was talking, I walked around to the far side of the room toward a small, dark doorway leading into the other upstairs section. I didn't make it far. My breath came harder and harder, and it wasn't from climbing the steps. *I can't breathe.* Slightly panicked at the heaviness now seeming to sit squarely on my sternum, I tried not to make a scene, so I leaned down, hands on my knees, waiting for the feeling to pass. Suddenly pictures started flashing in my head. They showed a shadowy shape running back and forth from the window to the cubbyholes in the wall.

"Are you okay?" asked another group member, catching sight of me.

"No," I gasped, trying to get air. "There's something here. It's telling me it watches and hides." I was tearing up now, a searing pain in my stomach and chest that was almost unbearable. I kept waiting for it to peak so I could make sense of what I was supposed to understand about this haunting.

I could see a little boy with blond hair and pajamas on. I knew his name was Christian, so I told my team members this. I was also getting the name Randall; he was making me feel pain in the stomach and chest area. He was also saying a name, *Lynn*. I informed my fellow investigators, and they wrote it down.

I straightened up a little, the pain from some past event I didn't as yet understand lessening with the verbal validation of its presence.

There were two small, square doors with latches at hip height in the room. The feelings were coming in strong here. I couldn't see anything near them; it was more a knowing that came over me.

"Something hides in these cubbyholes. It runs and changes positions, hiding in each of them. Something watches the house on the hill, through this window." I walked to the window that faced the house on the hill. *Yes, this window*, the little voice in my head told me again. Even through the rain, the big house on the hill could be seen clearly, looming over us.

"There's a bad feeling, and it's all coming from the direction of that house up there." I inclined my head toward the big house. "Something here is afraid of something there. Or something here watches to keep tabs on things there."

My friend Brian nodded, and a team member duly recorded the psychic impressions. As we went through the house, whenever I sensed residual energy of the past, I was given confirmation when I hit upon an accurate name or feeling.

"The little boy who lived here most recently was named Christian," Brian informed me. "He was terrified to stay in the upstairs and said there was a man who came. The girls who grew up here slept in this back room, and every night, they shoved their dresser up against the cubbyhole. Then in the morning, the dresser would be shoved away, and the cubby door would be open. It terrified them."

More information started coming to me. Someone named Karen was coming through now too.

"Karen was a favorite aunt who recently passed away," one of the investigators confirmed.

As I walked slowly around through the two rooms upstairs, I passed a spot at the far end near the doorway and sensed a strong negative force.

"Oh, something right here is very strong, very negative energy," I told them as I stood beside it. Brian decided to go downstairs and ask what had occurred at that spot. I waited, trying to make sense of the feelings coming from this innocent-looking empty space. There was only the open hardwood floor. Brian trotted back up the steps a few moments later with the owner and solved the mystery.

"That spot is where my sisters had one of their twin beds when we were growing up. They sat right there and played with a Ouija board," the owner said. Brian and I just looked at each other, and the owner returned downstairs to wait. Who knows what portal could've been opened. The residual vibe, at the very least, was still there. It takes knowledge of protection methods to safely use a Ouija board.

We descended to the first floor and did a walk-through of the bedrooms, and I experienced a sense of something that stood and watched the owner sleep. This was a creepy sort of shadow-man in my mind's eye. Then we walked into the basement. Here there was a sense of someone battling alcoholism. I also felt a grandfather's presence in several of the items on the walls, and this was confirmed.

I was relieved that so much came through for this family, but there was obviously something still unaccounted for. The terrible fear continuing to grip me came from that big house on the hill, less than fifty yards away. It was a fear I didn't yet understand. I knew it must be the missing puzzle piece, and I hoped it would be solved. This was the very reason I had finally embraced psychic abilities—to help others. I hoped I might be the one to solve it. But as soon as I heard the owner's story, everything became crystal clear.

―――――――

We finished downstairs, returned one last time to the upper floor for a final look, and then met with the family members who'd been waiting quietly in the kitchen. My investigator friend Brian left the digital voice recorder running as we talked with them, as he often does. His theory that a spirit will often join in conversations among others has proven true in the past. Brian explained what we had found so far in their house.

"Debra has come up with some accurate things, such as names you gave me in advance. There is also some information that still needs to be discovered. You guys may be able to tell us what some of Debra's psychic information means." We spoke with the family members for a few more minutes. I explained to them how sometimes using a Ouija will open things up in a home, paranormally speaking. I finished by saying that using a Ouija unprotected "is not a good idea, usually." I told the owners what I'd sensed upstairs and the names I'd been given clairaudiently. And then the family began to tell us about the site's history.

An Indian massacre resulting in the deaths of many settlers long ago had taken place near the left side of the little house. A church and parsonage had also stood on that spot a century after the massacre. None of this resonated very strongly with me, however, although the massacre may have been some of what I'd been feeling about hiding and chaos. Then the family began to tell us another story, and as soon as they did, it finally began to make sense.

"We found out something bizarre when we were kids," said the older daughter. She looked toward the big house on the hill, motioning toward it. "Long ago, an older couple lived up there. And the wife's brother lived in the little brown house on the other side of it." Her younger sister joined in. "The brother wasn't quite right, from what we heard. There was just something sort of off about him." Her elder sister agreed and proceeded to explain that the old couple and the woman's brother lived up there during their grandparents' generation. When their parents bought the house, the old couple was long dead, and one of their sons had inherited the big house. He was about the same age as their parents, and they all played with this man's kids, who were the grandkids of the original old couple.

One summer day, their family and the neighbors were all out back in their adjoining yards. Their neighbors on the hill had begun tearing down their old outhouse in the backyard, between their two yards. The eldest sister took up the story again.

"Our mom and dad were helping them. The men were smashing up the outhouse, and then digging out all the muck underneath. It was a dirty job. We were kids of course, not paying much attention, only half listening and running around the yard. But suddenly, we heard all the commotion stop over there."

Obviously, something had drawn the kids' attention to make them stop and go look. The kids went closer and stood there, staring. Everyone was frozen in place. One of their dads had pulled out a very long bone—obviously a human leg bone, a femur. The adults had all stared at each other, and then their mothers shooed the kids away. The sister paused for a moment, remembering, and told me they'd found out more the next day from their friends who lived next door—their parents broke down and told them the truth. The sister thought maybe their parents hadn't really believed the story themselves when *their* parents told *them*—at least not until they found the leg bone that day.

The neighbor's mother told her kids that one night, her uncle, the strange man who'd lived in the little brown house beside the big house when her parents lived there, brought a woman home. And for whatever reason, he killed her there. Their childhood friends didn't know if their grandma had found the woman or what had happened. But instead of calling the cops when they found this dead woman, the old couple stuffed the woman's body down the outhouse. And then they locked the grandma's crazy brother in the little brown house. They fed him through a hole in the door. And there the crazy brother stayed, imprisoned, until he died. As the current owner finished telling us investigators the story, all of us adult team members gathered in their kitchen stared at each other in shocked silence.

My mind was racing with the thoughts of what I'd felt and sensed. *So, the spirit of that poor murdered woman, the spirit of the crazy locked-up brother, and the spirits of that old couple, burdened by their terrible secret—they're probably all still here*…And someone's daughter, someone's mother or wife, went missing long ago, and no one ever knew what happened to her. It was *her* I was feeling—her terror. For all anyone knew, the murdered woman might've broken away from the strange man and tried to hide, then was found by him and finished off. Maybe that was the running, hiding, watching, sensation I kept getting.

The one thing I *do* know for sure, that woman is still there, and she is still terrified. I could feel her.

Later, I checked around, carefully and anonymously, just trying to see if there were any outstanding missing persons from that area from years ago, but that search has been inconclusive so far. I know the murdered woman wants to be remembered, to be acknowledged. I can feel her trying to gently remind me to tell her story. So far, I haven't found the answers, or a way to help her. But I'm still looking. I wish I could've gotten into the big house on the hill or the little brown house beside it. I'd have liked to stand inside, maybe get a better glimpse of which spirit was still there. I believe the evil brother is definitely there, and I also sense the murdered woman is too. I don't think she can rest until she has some sort of justice.

Our investigation wrapped things up there at the haunted house, and we thanked the owners, telling them we would follow up with whatever evidence we'd recorded.

————

After the investigation I was exhausted, just completely wrung out, as I often am when I use psychic abilities. It wears me out in a way that's a combination of mental and physical—maybe because I have to open myself completely and strain to hear and feel what's not obvious in a normal mind state. I guess it's a psychical strain. It's the reason I've never liked to take on events that require lots of readings in a row. Sometimes it causes a severe headache afterward. And I felt the stirrings of a bad one.

It was still raining as I backed out of the driveway of the haunted house. I sighed as I dug one-handed for the Aleve in my purse on the passenger seat and swallowed one down with my bottle of water. That night I planned a quiet evening at home with a cup of my favorite chai tea. I hoped to lose myself in a good book too. I didn't want to think about the investigation or psychic things at all; I'd had enough for one day.

As I drove home in the rain, my thoughts drifted to my son, James, as they invariably do. The story of the little boy Christian, who was so scared living at his haunted house, brought back the memories of James at that same age, dealing with our own home's spirits. I remembered how scared James had been the night he came running to me, telling me he'd seen people standing around a coffin in our foyer. It was too much for a little boy to grasp; a scene from the distant past playing out before him. Then my thoughts came full circle again; James being gone still seemed impossible and unreal, and the idea that he could come back as a spirit no less so.

My investigator friend Brian called me the next day with confirmations and a few EVPs. EVP is short for electronic voice phenomena, voices captured from the spirit world that are outside the range of human ears, but picked up on digital voice recorders. The sister of the man who lived at the haunted house, Lyn, had been very ill with pain where I'd felt it. Her father Randall had also died of cancer there. That day, I think he'd been showing me their pain, which had just about doubled me over. But I was left with a deep sense of unease at the EVPs the digital recorders caught. While I was downstairs talking with the family, explaining what I'd felt upstairs and confirming the names I'd received, I also mentioned their Ouija usage.

As I listened to the playback of me explaining to the family that "it's not a good idea to play with a Ouija, usually," you can hear what sounds like a pig grunting, just as I say "usually." Brian then played an enhanced and cleaned-up version of it. My blood ran cold as I heard a deep male voice saying "usually" right along with me—almost mocking me—except both voices sound as though they were coming from *me*. There was literally no delay—the "usually" was said right in time with me. I sounded like something out of *The Exorcist*! This frightened me, and my mind began to dart around for rational explanations. How could something so accurately anticipate what I was going to say? Enough so as to say it at exactly the same time that I did? Is this "something" what has followed me for so long? Was it *beside* me or *inside* me? And now the final question was raised in my mind. Could whatever this thing is be the cause of my lifetime of "extraordinary gifts?"

This scared me badly enough to try a technique I'd heard about. That night, I stood in front of the mirror to exorcise myself. *Okay, what's next? Because now you're just a few cats short of being a crazy cat lady.* I stared into my own eyes. I prayed, asking in God's name for anything evil to be cast out. I did this passionately, renouncing any hold the demonic might have over me. I know how crazy it sounds, but hearing that creepy evil voice seemingly coming out of my own mouth was a bit too much to take. Then I went to bed, and as I lay there in the dark, I closed my eyes and, asking to see something, began waiting for the pictures that usually come when I do readings, pictures that foretell the future or the health conditions of whoever I'm doing a reading for. Nothing. I tried again with the same result. Now I was worried. Maybe this psychic ability I'd thought was prophecy, a spiritual gift, was caused by evil and I'd just cast it out! I walked back into the bathroom and stared at myself again in the mirror. I searched my own face, my hairline, then came back to my eyes, and shook my head at the ridiculousness of it all. *Crazy cat lady!*

By the next day, I could see the clairvoyant pictures formed by the light again—so I knew it was just my own neurotic fears that had scared it out of me temporarily. In the rational light of day, I thought more about the voice on the EVP and realized it probably wasn't coming from me but rather was something matching me very closely as I spoke. Still, it was unnerving, and it hit a bit too close to home, playing upon my lifelong fears. It also made me more determined than ever to research whatever strange entity or slip of the digital recorder could cause such a thing. I was still dealing with the deaths of my father and my son, and their returns. Somehow, the trigger moment of hearing that eerie voice coming out of me set me on a new mission to somehow understand it all.

———

I thought I'd already discovered everything I possibly could during my life-changing journey after the deaths of my son and my father. But maybe there was still more to know. I was determined to find out once and for all.

I decided to put the word out, and I began to call all the friends who'd told me their strange stories about their loved ones' returns after death. The more I thought about my son James's returns, the more I wanted to compare my experiences with others to find any possible connections. I had also experienced a wealth of evidence on paranormal investigations and so had my investigator friends. Whether it was a loved one's return or a more random ghostly occurrence, I felt that if I could only hear enough stories, maybe I could piece together some universal truth. Maybe some sort of epiphany, some light bulb moment would strike and help me understand my own situation. But deep down I also recognized that I might not ever want to stop chasing this elusive understanding until I truly knew something for sure. Because of this, I didn't know if I could ever stop.

I began collecting ghost stories from my friends, family, and paranormal investigators, sorting them into various categories, such as intelligent hauntings; the returns of loved ones or spirits who tried to communicate; residual hauntings, those that recurred over and over like a tape loop; and, finally, unspecified hauntings. Some of those might be poltergeist-like in nature, or even demonic, depending on how I labeled the intent behind them.

I went about my daily life as I gathered these stories, fitting people's interviews between my music performances, investigations, and writing. And I found stories everywhere, some very close to home.

2

BEYOND THE VEIL

Many of my numerous haunted experiences are detailed in my first book. Some of the crazy things I'd witnessed since moving in to a haunted house as a teen made me reevaluate what I'd been taught. I realized there was much more out there in the world than we were being told, and that's when I first vowed to understand it.

Spirits tried desperately to get my attention in that first haunted house. They scratched on my sheets while I lay in bed. They touched me, locked me in the bathroom, even dumped a visiting adult male out of a heavy upholstered chair! I didn't know then that I could set some ground rules—I was so terrified, I could barely acknowledge that there *were* spirits, let alone speak out loud to them!

This began my life focused on the paranormal. In my spare time, music filled any other void, eventually becoming my full-time job. Finally, my understanding of this first haunting came full circle when I found the 1940 census for the haunted house on Fifth Street. My great-grandmother's son lived in the house then. He would've been my grandpa's first cousin. Suddenly it seemed as though family spirits might have been trying to contact me. But I certainly didn't understand this at that young age. And it nearly traumatized me for life.

————

The old red-brick buildings glowed with the warmth of the setting sun as I unloaded my guitar and equipment in Roscoe Village. The beautiful little canal town, restored to early 1800s glory, hosted two of my regular playing venues. I've been a professional musician almost as long as I've been a psychic—and I was born psychic. Uncorked, the wine bar where I was performing that night, had been many things during its century-and-a-half existence, even a morgue. Its newest owners were Joe and Lorrie, who had been my friends for years, ever since they'd hired me to play music at their previous business.

I'd occasionally used Uncorked's back party room to do psychic readings for clients in town. I'd just given readings to a group there a few days before. As I carried my guitar in, I passed a table with a man and two women. They stopped me.

"Hey," the man said. "I'm sorry I had to cancel my reading appointment at the last minute." I smiled at all three of the friends as I switched to psychic mode temporarily, remembering that someone a few days before had canceled.

I told him it was okay, that it happened sometimes. Suddenly a name was whispered in my head. *Kenny.* "Who's Kenny?" I asked him. Both girls' sharp intake of breath told me I'd hit upon something.

"Oh my God, we were just talking about him! Not two minutes before you came in," cried one girl. She explained that she'd been telling the man with her about Kenny, a mutual acquaintance of theirs, who'd been giving her a hard time recently. She'd wanted his advice.

I told them how sometimes I just picked things up like that. The man, still looking slightly startled, told me he'd reschedule very soon. I smiled, and promptly switched back to music mode. I was getting pretty used to doing this by now. It happened a lot.

Most of the time, Joe, the co-owner of Uncorked and a fellow musician, joined me onstage when I played there. After our second set, we sat at a large table talking with friends, and the subject of hauntings came up. Joe had previously told a few stories about some unexplainable events in the building. Several times, I even thought I'd felt something myself while in the restrooms. That night, since it was a little slower than usual due to a storm, I asked Joe if he'd take me into the basement—the former morgue—to see what I could sense. I've always noticed that rain seems to be more conducive to spirits. Perhaps because water is a very efficient conductor of electrical energy, and most believe spirit energy is electrical in nature.

"Sure, let's go," Joe said with a smile. He opened the door right across from where we'd been sitting, and I followed him down a steep set of wooden stairs as he told me a story.

"*I've* never seen too much here, which is just the way I like it, by the way." Joe laughed over his shoulder. "Lorrie hasn't been so lucky though." We reached the bottom of the stairs and the walls consisted of gigantic hand-hewn stone blocks with pick marks on them, common to the era almost two centuries ago.

One night the bar was busy upstairs, and Lorrie ran down to get a bottle of something. She saw Joe just ahead of her as he turned the corner into the next room, and she started talking to him, asking Joe to grab a bottle of wine for her. Then she turned the corner and no one was there. She'd clearly seen a dark, pants leg and lighter shirt on a man's form rounding the corner and just assumed it was Joe. Just then, she heard someone start down the steps behind her—*that* was Joe. Lorrie was pretty upset.

"No wonder she doesn't like to come down here alone," I told Joe. Lorrie had just mentioned that fact to me earlier that night.

As I walked through the basement, I could sense certain hotspots—places where the psychic vibe was strong and there was some sort of lingering residual energy or presence. I pointed out a couple of these places to Joe. I decided to speak out loud to whoever might be listening. I sensed shyness or fear from them, like they were holding back, just quietly watching us.

"I can feel you here," I told them. "Don't be afraid. Joe and Lorrie are the new owners now, and they're good people. You have nothing to fear from them—or from me." I stood quietly listening, but there were no answering sounds, nothing to give away the presence I knew was hiding there.

Joe showed me through the rest of the basement, then we made our way back upstairs and finished playing our last set of music. I didn't think too much about it at the time, but I soon heard from Joe. He wasn't too thrilled about the results of my little talk with the spirits at Uncorked in Roscoe Village.

"Man, you sure stirred something up," he told me a few weeks later. "I was there alone one night, getting ready to close. I was standing behind the last two customers, who were sitting at the bar. My arms were folded across my chest, like so." He crossed his arms to show me. "All three of us were watching the game. Suddenly, someone lifted my elbow up about four inches." Joe raised his elbow, arms still crossed, to show me what he meant. "Someone invisible! I've never been so scared in my life." Joe said he got the hell out of there and didn't really want to go back! But obviously, since it's his business, he had to.

This does happen sometimes. I believe that after I talked to the spirits at Uncorked, they knew someone could sense them and was acknowledging them. And maybe someone even cared enough to explain who the owners were. They felt understood. After seeing Joe there with me in the basement, they must've felt close to him as well. Close enough to make their presence known to Joe that night they lifted up his arm, much like an old friend would. But Joe did *not* want to be friends and he was *not* amused.

"I don't want them touching me or showing up here when I'm alone. It's just not good!" Joe shook his head, and I explained how to talk to them himself; just speak out loud and set some rules. Like the people they once were, they understood rules.

I told Joe he just had to tell the invisible residents that he didn't want to be surprised by them. This is what I've had to do in my own house over the years. It's always worked for me. I gave him some background on my haunted house, and he seemed relieved. The next time I saw Joe, he told me it had worked so far, although one night he set a bottle on the bar, and when he turned around, it had been moved carefully to the floor.

"That, I can take," he said, laughing. "It was a far cry from picking up my elbow that first night! I guess they just didn't want that bottle set on 'their' bar at that moment, and they wanted to let me know!"

Joe continues to talk to the ghosts at Uncorked, and they seem to listen—just as James seems to listen to me.

Not too long after Joe's talk with the spirits in Uncorked, he and Lorrie invited me to hold a book signing there. It turned into a fun day, with many friends stopping by to say hi, buy books, and eat a cookie or three. After everyone left, I packed up and was walking across the patio outside when someone called my name. I turned to see an old friend seated at an outdoor table with her husband. This was a lady who'd had many readings with me. I hadn't seen her for a while and we hugged.

"I'm so glad to see you," she said, spying my box of books. "And I want to buy some books too!"

I signed both of my books for her, and we filled each other in on what we'd been up to since the last time we'd talked. Her husband offhandedly picked up my fiction title, *Sarah's Shadows*, which has a picture of a ghost on the cover. "I think I know what *this* one is about," he joked.

I laughed and told him it's what they *all* were about! My friend glanced at her husband, then back at me and told me her husband didn't used to believe in that stuff.

"Really? And he does now?" Her husband nodded, and I asked him what had happened to change his mind.

A couple weeks earlier, they'd been sitting out on the patio facing the street, when someone came up behind him and slapped the back of his head pretty hard. He just figured it was Joe or one of his other friends playing around. When he turned around to see who it was, no one was there. That really freaked him out. I thought about my musician friend Joe, the owner of the bar. Maybe his talk with the spirits drove them outside to pick on unsuspecting customers! My friend's husband continued telling me about his experience that day.

"Then when I went in to the restroom, the door to the urinal slowly swung open. After that, I was pretty nervous. I even checked the stall door—it was level; it did not move or swing open on its own. I can now honestly say I'm a little less skeptical!" He rubbed the back of his head, as though still feeling that slap, a slightly worried expression on his face.

I was familiar with the odd feeling in the ladies' room. The women's restroom definitely has a heavy vibe. It has always creeped people out. I talked with the couple for a little while longer, then we said our goodbyes and I headed home. I wondered about the restroom areas, which held both the men's and women's, side by side. What might lurk there? I've never seen anything there, but I sure can feel it. And I know others who have had things happen to them there too. Joe just might have to have another talk with his spirits—and tell them not to approach patrons at their most vulnerable moments. And no slapping allowed!

3

SCHOOL FOR GHOSTS

My cousin Joyce called one night and asked me to come out to the edge of town to her workplace. She'd been a longtime volunteer at our local genealogical society and had taken on the job of archiving and microfilming a huge stockpile of wills and death records for our county. These records were stored in the basement of the county's old nursing home mostly because there was no room for them anywhere else, and some were getting damaged. The genealogical society was working to have all county records compiled electronically before they were lost forever. Though in transition, the county home still served as a nursing home for a few elderly and disabled indigent residents. The basement, however, had long since been abandoned, except for the farthest room in the back: the laundry room.

My cousin Joyce and I have always been close. She's a few years younger, but because our dads were brothers and our moms were sisters, we had all the same relatives on both sides. So we've always felt closer than just cousins—more like sisters. Joyce has shared my interest in the paranormal almost her entire life, and she also inherited the family artistic streak; mine leaned toward music and hers toward art. She's a talented artist, and these days Joyce creates delightfully eerie art dolls. They call this Halloween Art, and it has a very large fan base of collectors. Joyce has experienced my psychic abilities firsthand and has a bit of the psychic streak herself.

I spent a lot of time with Joyce when we were younger, experimenting with my own psychic abilities, trying to both define and understand them. She helped me practice sending and receiving clairvoyant messages back then. Joyce would look at a random picture in a magazine, and I would tell her what I was seeing in my head. One time, she picked up a magazine with an advertisement of a baby lying on its back in a crib with its feet up in the air. The baby's feet were foremost in the picture and enlarged in the camera's eye. At the time, I had a pin I wore on my coat—a pair of tiny silver feet. I told Joyce that what I was seeing looked like the pin on my coat.

We realized then that a direct hit like that proves that I was reading Joyce's mind telepathically. After this, I was always cautious when seeing any clairvoyant picture, always careful to discern whether the information was something that I could pick up by mind-reading—something already accessible in that person's thoughts. If not, I knew it was truly coming from a source other than myself. This has caused confusion over the years, and for a long time, I wondered if clairvoyance was coming from some outside force—namely, a spirit or even something evil. After much research and debate, I finally decided it was a spiritual gift. But until I did, it gave me a lot of torment. Even now, I still have the occasional moments of doubt. I still experiment too, using myself as a guinea pig.

When I answered the phone, I was glad to hear Joyce's voice.

"I'm hearing noises," Joyce told me, "and I really don't like the vibe down there, at all! I'm all by myself, and it's really creepy! Please come visit me, okay?" Joyce usually had an assistant with her, but the next day she said she'd be there alone.

"Okay, but don't tell me anything else about the place. I want to see what I can sense on my own."

Joyce agreed, and I told her I'd be there at 2:00 the next day.

As I drove to the edge of town, the old county home could be seen from quite a distance. It sprawled majestically on a knoll off to my left. Built of red brick, with a center section and two enormous wings stretching out to each side, it was a handsome old building. I thought I remembered hearing that the original building dated to the 1840s, with sections added on every so often. A long, curving blacktopped driveway snaked up the hill to a parking lot in front. Joyce had told me to come around to the left-hand side, to a door that was tucked neatly into the corner of the south wing where it met the main building. I looked at my watch; 2:00 exactly.

Just as I took the sidewalk around the building, Joyce appeared. "You made it, fantastic!"

I was always happy to see my little sister/cousin, and we talked as we approached the door to the basement.

I asked her what was going on there, since she sounded so upset the night before.

Joyce laughed nervously and told me there were some stories there that were pretty weird. Joyce pulled open the basement door. "Just tell me what *you* feel down here," she said.

We descended into an area that had seen better days; old paint peeled from the walls, and as I walked in, I saw a few of the smaller rooms showed streaks from water damage where it had run down below the window wells. Initially, I saw many small rooms along the corridor, and I stopped beside one that had the strongest psychic sensations to it.

This first room had a pretty strong vibe—I sensed chaos, fear, and lots of bad stuff. A bench lined one wall, which was painted an industrial green, and the paint above the bench was peeling away in strips. I told Joyce what I was feeling.

Joyce nodded and told me this was where they brought patients in: the intake room. The building had been an infirmary, a poor house, and a nursing home—sometimes even taking in mental patients; it had been lots of different things over the years. Joyce told me that sometimes, if someone was mentally handicapped and upset, they would leave them here in this little room for hours until they could evaluate them. I could sense a lot of negativity in that one small room.

We moved down the hall to where Joyce was set up. It wasn't in much better shape than what I'd seen so far— more peeling paint, crumbling walls, water damage, and dirt on the cement floors. Joyce told me she found some dead mice in there too, which, knowing her, would have been bad enough! She had a small desk and a chair set up in the middle of the room. One tiny window let in a little bit of light, and a bare bulb hung suspended from the ceiling. Under the window, tables against the wall held box after crumbling box of papers: the old county records.

"This *is* pretty creepy," I admitted, looking up at the ceiling. I could discern weird vibes coming from all around. And Joyce had been down here every day! My unease was apparent and Joyce gave a little shiver in the dank room. She walked to the doorway and pointed into the dark recesses of the hallway past her room. "Come back here. I want to see if you feel anything."

Joyce stepped aside, allowing me to lead the way, and I opened up to the sensations I was getting. A strong sense of something dark drew me deeper into the building, and we passed more small rooms until finally we came to a large one that appeared to run almost the length of the main structure. I had a sensation of fear, and yet it was mixed with hatred as well. *This is where it's coming from.* I stopped, feeling a presence in the dim room. I suddenly pinpointed it. *It's over in that far corner, behind those old dryers.* I squinted into the shadows—I couldn't see anything, but I could sure feel it! The room was very quiet. "Who's back there?" I called tentatively. I took a step forward, then another. A thick, black wall of rage took my breath away for a moment, and, terrified, I stopped. *It's going to get me!*

"Something's in that back corner," I stage-whispered to Joyce. She nodded, wrapping her arms around herself. I backed up suddenly, wanting out of there. "Let's go," I said hurriedly, still walking backwards, not wanting to take my eyes off whatever was in the corner. I still couldn't see anything. But I could certainly feel it. When we got to the hall, I turned and we both sped back to the relative safety of Joyce's room—which suddenly felt warm and welcoming, peeling paint and all!

"I just knew you'd feel something…you pinpointed exactly where they heard it."

"Heard what?" I expelled the breath I'd been holding in a whoosh. "All right, tell me what you know!"

"Let's get out of here," Joyce said. She inclined her head toward the exit and said she needed a smoke.

We climbed the stairs, and she told me there had been a lot of noises since she'd been working there. We headed back up into the sunshine while Joyce began to talk, relaying the story she'd just heard from one of the few remaining employees in the nursing home above.

Joyce had finally felt driven to tell a few of the workers about what she'd been hearing: things moving, thumps, scraping sounds—and one of the kitchen workers told her a story that really scared her.

The people who worked there heard a lot of noises too, and none of them ever wanted to come to the basement to do the laundry. There were only a few residents left, but the workers still had to take care of them and wash the bed linens. One of these ladies broke down and told Joyce the story that scared her so badly.

One night in the 1950s, a nurse's aide came down to do the laundry, and she could hear the sound of heavy breathing coming from the corner I'd pointed to. This worker ran to get her supervisor because there were a few residents there who were mentally handicapped—and some were violent. The worker figured one had probably gotten out of their room and was hiding in the basement. The supervisor returned with some backup, and they all carefully called for the patient to come out, reassuring him that they wouldn't hurt him, and so on. But the supervisor couldn't coax anyone out. Finally, the nursing supervisor went back upstairs to do a headcount, to try to ascertain exactly who was hiding in the basement and whether they were violent or not.

After the headcount, the supervisor found that no one was missing upstairs. At that point, she decided to call the local police, thinking maybe some derelict had broken in and was hiding down there.

The cops arrived to find the supervisor in the parking lot waiting for them, and she explained that there was someone in the basement hiding behind the dryers. The police went down the basement stairs with guns drawn and stood quietly, listening in the large laundry room. They too could hear the steady, strained breathing, rasping and wheezing, in and out, heavily. Joyce took a drag of the cigarette as I waited in suspense. Finally, she continued her story.

The cops slowly approached the corner and made their move into the space behind the dryers. But nothing was there. Then they searched everywhere else in the room. There was nothing there either. Joyce exhaled cigarette smoke. "The place was empty. Yet that heavy breathing sound went on and on."

The baffled cops finally left, seriously disturbed by the loud breathing coming from the room with no human being there to cause it. After that first time, the same thing happened several more times, and the same scenario was repeated—the nurses called about heavy breathing in the basement, the cops came out, and nothing could be found. The local cops knew what to expect after a while. It was always the same when they came; loud breathing in that back corner of the basement laundry room. But nobody was ever found there.

"Oh my lord," I whispered. "I could feel it back there, but I don't know what it is."

"Thank God I'll be done microfilming soon," Joyce whispered. "I just don't want to be in there anymore."

"I don't blame you." I was glad to get out of there, to be honest.

Joyce walked me to my car and I felt bad leaving her there, but relieved that I was going. What a creepy place!

Not too long after, the last of the residents were moved elsewhere, and the building was sold to a university. I believe the only classes they should hold there are ghost hunting classes—because there's *definitely* something to hunt!

4

THEY DON'T MEAN TO STARE

My ghost hunting friend Brian Fain, founder of MGHS (Massillon Ghost Hunters Society), has been interested in the afterlife since he was a child. I've found this is true of most of us paranormal enthusiasts, both professional investigators and armchair ghost hunters alike. But what stands out most about Brian is that he founded MGHS in 2004—long before the paranormal craze had begun. In fact, he organized MGHS the month before the TAPS show was first aired. As most of us who've followed the rising popularity of ghost hunting know, TAPS was the TV show that first brought ghost hunting to public awareness in a huge way.

Brian's wife and several family members formed the core group of MGHS at first. After Brian got his first digital voice recorder, he decided to go to Massillon Cemetery, a huge burial ground with more than twenty thousand bodies interred, a literal city of the dead. That first trip, Brian and his wife Lena walked through the beautiful grounds, which were covered with fall leaves. They began to notice what sounded like another person following them—the crunching of the leaves under an extra set of feet! The couple motioned to each other, synchronized their steps, stopped simultaneously, and sure enough, *crunch, crunch* followed them. Brian had brought a small camera and started walking again, then wheeled around and snapped a picture. After the film was developed, the image displayed a large mist right behind them. It was a clear day, and nothing could explain this anomaly.

Brian could also hear a faint voice when he played back his recorder, but he couldn't make it out. Both of these bits of evidence were intriguing, but not enough to pass muster with Brian. So he decided to go back for more. This time, his sister-in-law Chris was with him. They spent time walking around and recording. Later on, listening to the playback, a voice could clearly be heard saying, "Chris, it's me." They were never able to figure out who this might have been. But it was enough to drive them forward in founding MGHS, and they began to refine their skills as a paranormal investigation group.

MGHS finally got their first haunted house case a year later after they'd gotten their website up and running. The woman who contacted them to investigate had a house that was more than one hundred and thirty years old, and it had been in her family all of those years.

The family had many experiences in the house. One night, the woman got up for a drink of water and heard someone walking in the hallway. She thought it was her husband, but she saw no one. One day when her daughter was six, the little girl pointed to the stairs and said, "Mom, who's that man?" The woman looked at the stairs and saw an old man with white hair and a long beard standing there. As they stared, the man disappeared before their eyes! Not long after that, the medicine cabinet door opened as she stood in front of it. The woman would also sometimes run into "somebody" in the hallway and experience a stiff shoulder bumping her back.

MGHS investigated the house, taking readings, temperatures, and EVP recordings. While the team was in the attic, which was filled with heirlooms, all three of their flashlights went out. Brian had just put fresh batteries in each one, so he knew something was draining the energy. Upon playback of the digital recorder, an EVP of a man's voice asks, "Who the heck is that?" Upstairs, a clear female voice was recorded saying, "They ain't cousins," as if in answer to the man! Could these voices be long-deceased family members recognizing that the MGHS team were strangers? It sure seemed that way. One other EVP was a female saying, "Help me." Getting this kind of evidence on their first major investigation was heady stuff.

Brian and another MGHS member met with the woman and her daughter, who had grown into a teenager, to give them their evidence. When Brian played the EVP of the man asking "Who the heck was that?" a huge sound came from upstairs. It felt as though a bowling ball had been dropped! All four of them sitting at the dining room table jumped—the reverberation was that loud. Brian asked the woman if her husband was home, and she said no. They all went upstairs expecting to see something big that had fallen over. It would definitely have to be big to create that amount of noise and vibration. Nothing was out of place, and no cats or people were upstairs. Nothing upstairs could've caused it. They all speculated that the man's spirit heard his voice being played back and in his shock, somehow created this huge sound. It was uncanny.

The woman's haunting came and went, with long spells of quiet in between, and as soon as the family would almost get used to the silence, the haunting would start once again with no rhyme or reason. So MGHS has kept in touch with the family over the years. The fledgling paranormal group's first case had proven to be a good one, and it only stoked their ghost hunting fire!

———

One cold day in October, Brian and two members of his group went to a cemetery in Canton, Ohio, to try to capture some EVPs. As Brian begins each EVP session, he usually makes an announcement. "The device you see in my hand will help us pick up evidence of your existence. It will pick up your voice on tape. So please come close and speak into the device." But it was too cold to stay very long, and on their way out, they passed by a headstone with the name Bye. As Brian passed it, he jokingly said, "bye," and Christine who followed him also called out, "bye." Finally, Brian's wife, Lena, the last one out, laughed and said "bye."

Half frozen, they made their way home and huddled around the recorder to hear the evidence. They hadn't recorded very long before the weather chased them away, but they listened carefully to what they had. Finally, they came to the end of their EVP session when each of them had said "bye." First Brian, then Christine, then Lena gave the name on the tombstone beside the exit. There was a small pause, and suddenly a fourth voice answered: "bye." The MGHS members jumped up from their chairs—four voices and only three of them were there!

The day after hearing the extra "bye" they'd caught on tape, Brian took his totally skeptical brother-in-law out to the cemetery. Brian's brother-in-law didn't believe they'd really caught anything; he believed someone else there had said "bye" twice. Once at the cemetery, they walked to some old mausoleums, and Brian stuck his head in one of the broken windows. Just then, his brother-in-law coughed and Brian jumped. "You scared me," laughed Brian.

When they got home to play back the day's recording, Brian's brother-in-law sat on the sofa with arms crossed in a "prove it" stance. The recorder picked up the sound of his brother-in-law's cough and then Brian saying that he'd scared him. Then a woman's voice says, "Leave us!" The formerly skeptical brother-in-law made Brian play this back a dozen times, simply in awe that an invisible woman—a spirit—was there with them at that moment. This was definitely the cure for his skepticism.

At another EVP session, Brian and a team member went to a cemetery to see what they could pick up. At another old mausoleum, the team member peered into the gap in the chained doors and asked a rhetorical question: "I wonder what's in there?" When they got home and played the tape back, a woman's voice is heard immediately after the question. She answers, "Nothing."

Sometimes it seems spirits are aware of their state. Another EVP was caught as Brian called out the name on a stone, which he sometimes did as he walked through, as a marker. A plaintive woman's voice can be heard clearly, answering, "I'm dead."

The same day the woman noted her deceased state, Brian recorded another voice. Just after Brian announced out loud in his usual fashion how they could capture the spirits' voices on tape if they would just try to speak to the investigators, a man's voice said, "I can't believe they're getting us on tape."

Another time at a cemetery, Brian read the names of the deceased from the headstones as he passed by. When they listened back, after a man's name is read, a woman's voice says, "Give him my love." Of course, no one knew who this might be, whether it was his wife speaking or not. But it does give one pause for thought: If his wife is there, and still needs to send him her love, where is he?

Ghost hunters don't always need to search the largest cemeteries to gather good evidence. Brian described an old Quaker cemetery with only twelve graves where the group asked a few questions of the residents.

"What is your name?" was the question that got an interesting reply. Upon playback, a little boy answers, "Timmy!" He sounded happy and excited, but soon after, a woman's voice is heard asking, "Why are you with them?" as if to show her disapproval. Perhaps Timmy was her young son and he'd run away from his mom to see what the investigators were doing. Apparently, even in the afterlife children get scolded!

This same small cemetery was the source of another interesting EVP. One day as Brian and his group moved among the stones asking questions, a neighbor came out of her house and walked over to them. She asked them if they'd like to have some more information on the old cemetery.

Of course, Brian was very interested, and the lady brought out a huge stack of old papers and files. In those days, record-keeping was shaky at best, and one of the articles about the old cemetery told of how it was too cold in the winter to bury the dead, as the ground was too hard—and so their bodies were kept in cellars or other places until the graves could be dug. Because of this, the dates of death were often wrong, since many bodies waited until the spring thaw before they were able to be buried. So if you died in December of one year, you may not have been buried until March of the following year. This apparently caused a mix-up of dates. That day, knowing this information proved helpful.

According to his usual practice, Brian read off the stone as a marker, showing where the group was. The stone was broken off, so in effect, this woman buried there was nameless. All that could be read was: "was buried with her two children." And below that, the date, 1811. On the recorder, following Brian's announcement of her death date, a woman's voice is clearly heard correcting him, immediately saying, "1810." Brian also recognized this woman's voice—it was the woman who'd scolded Timmy for going over to the ghost hunters! It seemed as though this may have been Timmy's mother, the lady buried with her two children, of whom Timmy may have been one.

At another cemetery, fifteen minutes into the EVP recording, a male's voice is heard saying, "Please come over here" in a desperate tone, as if he really wanted to talk to someone. Unfortunately, EVPs are hard to check in real time, so his plea wasn't heard until they'd gone home hours later. Brian checks in on these disembodied voices/spirits at various times during the year, and I believe he may have built a rapport with them over time.

A reassuring spirit was caught on an EVP from Massillon Cemetery on a day when all six team members were present. Brian happened to look up and notice the groundskeepers, the custodians, and several others staring at their group as the team members made their way among the graves. Brian's niece then made the comment, "Look, they're staring at us." The MGHS members smiled and waved in the direction of the curious cemetery employees, always friendly and professional in their pursuit of the paranormal. Once at home, having downloaded the audio from the day, a class A EVP was captured at that very moment. A little girl's voice rings out in answer, saying, "They don't mean to stare." I bet her mother had taught her manners well, and the girl was giving the caretakers the benefit of the doubt!

MGHS chooses to post only class A EVPs (clear and easily understandable voices) on their website, or solid class Bs (audible, but not entirely clear), and these can all be heard at www.massillonghosthunters.com.

5

IT'S STILL 1782

My area of northeast Ohio has a rich history full of folk-lore and hauntings. Both spirits and legends come together here in Ohio's first settlement, a town called Schoenbrunn (pronounced "Shunbrun"). The town was founded in 1772 by Christian missionaries and their Delaware Indian converts, who had embraced Christianity and the white man's ways. This didn't save them though—a decade later, a band of American militia massacred them all one night after finding the bloody dress of a slain settler that had been planted by a hostile (unconverted) Indian.

The ninety-six mutilated bodies of the men, women, and children lay where they fell. After the mass murder, Indian war parties passed by Schoenbrunn hurriedly, and white men shunned it as well. The entire valley was considered haunted. First came the story of an army that camped among the ruins of the town one night, exhausted from fighting and marching. They fled in horror before dawn broke, claiming that during a thunderstorm they saw the apparition of a grotesque Indian witch leading the skeletons of the murdered victims.

Another story came from a party of warriors returning from a raid. They stopped at Schoenbrunn for water from the spring. On their belts were the scalps and tongues of the men, women, and children they'd killed. As they leaned over to drink, they saw their victims' faces reflected in the water. Then the dried tongues of their victims dangling from their belts began to moan and wail. The warriors fled in terror.

The remains of the massacred victims lay strewn about the site of their demise for a long time. Eventually, all trace of the town was lost, grown over by the forest. Years later, during a survey, the bones of the victims were found again and interred in a common grave. But it wasn't until almost a century later that a monument was built and dedicated to the victims. As if the massacre wasn't bad enough, the disrespect to the victims' earthly remains probably was. This has historically caused numerous hauntings elsewhere.

Eventually, replicas of the cabins were rebuilt upon the original sites, and it became a beautiful, peaceful setting. It also became a popular tourist destination. The log cabins and vegetable gardens are laid out in an orderly fashion, but there are still a few disorderly spirits here in Schoenbrunn.

My friend Sherri Brake, author and owner of Haunted Heartland Tours, held a ghost hunting event at Schoenbrunn Village a few summers ago, and I was excited to be a part of it. Sherri's events give small groups the chance to investigate various venues, everything from haunted prisons to abandoned institutions. These haunted events are very popular and sell out quickly, sometimes within minutes. Patrons can wander for hours at a time and sometimes even stay overnight at certain locations. Schoenbrunn was a new venue for Sherri, and it was a chance to investigate the village by lantern and flashlight. I couldn't wait.

I set up a table to do readings for attendees in the main-entrance building, which also housed a museum. When I was finished with my list of readings, I walked through the village, exploring the rebuilt cabins. It was a beautiful, warm summer night with a partial moon. The lanterns cast eerie shapes and elongated our shadows on the paths that ran in front of the restored log buildings.

I caught sight of Sherri across the wide grass concourse between the two rows of cabins and walked over to tell her I'd wrapped up for the night. I also told her I thought I'd do a little investigating myself. Sherri smiled and nodded.

"Well, I can tell you the spirits are out tonight," she said, shaking her head.

Instantly curious, I asked what had happened.

Turns out that a group of ladies stopped Sherri during the course of the evening and asked if she'd show them how to do an EVP session.

EVP stands for electronic voice phenomena, and a session consists of a person asking a question or series of questions out loud while using a digital voice recorder, then waiting about fifteen seconds between each question so the entity has a chance to reply. After a few minutes, the person then listens to the playback to see if any disembodied voices responded to them. Many times, spirits will be heard answering on the voice recorder. Supposedly, spirit voices are below the audible range of our hearing, but can be picked up electronically. I've captured many EVPs myself. A class A EVP is a clear and understandable voice, with class B being less so, and so on.

Sherri took the ladies into what is known as the Davis cabin and they all sat on the floor, with only the weak glow from the lantern to see their surroundings. So it was a little spooky to begin with. Then Sherri explained how to wait between asking the questions to give a spirit time to answer you. Sherri first demonstrated it for the three ladies, asking, "Is there anybody in here with us?" She waited the fifteen seconds or so, then shut the recorder off and played it back. First, Sherri's voice was heard, asking if there was anybody in there with them, and then a deep male voice answered, "Yes!" The ladies screeched, jumped up, and ran out—one of them calling back over her shoulder, "I've heard enough." Of course, there were only four *women* in that cabin, and it was obviously a *man's* spirit speaking to them. Sherri chuckled as she told me, "I never saw anyone move so fast!" Several others had also reported things happening to them that night. The spirits were definitely active!

These curious ladies, first-time ghost hunters, were very excited to try their hand at it, but they got a bit more than they'd bargained for at Schoenbrunn.

6

BALONEY

I met Darrin Troyer and his wife at another of Sherri Brake's events, this one a haunted presentation at a library. Darrin had formed his ghost hunting group, the Amish Paranormal Society (www.amishparanormalsociety.com), not long before. Although Darrin himself isn't Amish, his great-grandmother had been, and the group's name was his little nod to his heritage. During the course of Sherri's program, she introduced me to her audience as a psychic she worked with occasionally. After the event concluded, Darrin sought me out.

Darrin told me he was a huge fan of Sherri's and went to a lot of her haunted events. He also said he owned a 101-year-old family business, Troyer's Trail Bologna, and noted that some strange things were happening at the factory. Darrin asked me if I might be interested in coming out to see what I could pick up.

Troyer's Trail Bologna is a regionally famous brand of smoked meat that is sold in a ring, much like some kinds of kielbasa. The delicious meat has recently gone nationwide after having been a regional staple in Ohio since I was a child. At most of our area's Christmas and holiday events, you are sure to find a tray of sliced Trail Bologna and Swiss cheese. It is still the go-to local snack food.

I told Darrin I'd be happy to come to his factory. We made small talk about my old love for Trail Bologna and his new love of ghost hunting. We set up a time, and a week later, my husband and I drove to the small town of Trail to visit Darrin's company. My investigator friend Brian and his wife Lena of Massillon Ghost Hunters Society, met us there.

When we walked in, the first thing I noticed was the wonderful aroma of Trail Bologna. The meat is smoked, and the smell pervaded the building. In fact, our clothing smelled of this long after we left! Darrin then introduced us to his mom, who was also interested in seeing what I picked up psychically. We talked for a few minutes in that first small workroom, and I was already sensing and hearing things. There was the steady sensation of a presence just behind me, over by a shiny steel table that looked like a workstation. And the name "Ray" was being whispered in my head clairaudiently.

I pointed at the empty area beside the steel table. "Someone is over there; he likes to play pranks." I walked toward the spot. "And there is someone named Ray too, but it's someone different." Darrin looked startled and told me his uncle had stood in that very spot at the steel table workstation for many years. Then he added that his uncle had passed away not too long ago. Darrin told me the new guy who worked in that spot now had been upset because someone kept flicking his ear and moving his things around—almost like they were playing pranks on him. Then Darrin added that his uncle was quite a prankster!

Darrin's mother confirmed his uncle's practical-jokester ways and then added another piece to the psychic puzzle when she told me, "I had a young nephew named Ray." Darrin's mom asked if I'd seen the small creek that ran past out front. She explained that there was a bridge that spanned it farther down. One year, the creek was swollen from spring rains and young Ray stood on the bridge, mesmerized by the rushing water. The family speculated that the boy became dizzy while staring at the fast-moving flow, lost his balance, fell in, and drowned. Ray's body was lost somewhere downstream. Darrin's dad then told them there was a strange tradition, sort of an old wives' tale, but it always worked to find a drowned body; you just put some bread into the water, and it would stop right above wherever the body had traveled to. So Darrin's dad put a piece of bread in the creek and tracked it, watching as it traveled downstream. It made the sharp right turn down at the end of the road and came to rest above an area almost a mile and a quarter away. The men pulled away some brush, and there they found young Ray's body wedged under it at that very spot.

I told Darrin I'd never heard of this before. Later on, I researched this and found a 1767 London *Gentleman's Magazine* telling of using bread infused with quicksilver to find a drowned body. An 1819 newspaper in Pennsylvania also documented a similar procedure, as did no less a personage than Mark Twain, who wrote about this method in his novel *The Adventures of Huckleberry Finn.*

Darrin led the way, and our little group began a walking tour through the factory. I gave my impressions as Darrin pointed out various areas. Darrin's mother stayed behind, seated comfortably in the front section as the rest of us walked deeper into the bowels of the building. We saw huge carcasses of beef hanging in coolers, traveled through smaller rooms equipped with tables and machines, and finally we came to a spot where I sensed a lot of movement—a sort of tossing motion, almost like a game of some kind. I stood at the spot where I felt this had been going on and showed Darrin what I sensed, swinging my arm as though throwing something. He laughed and then pointed to a place on the floor where my imaginary trajectory would have landed whatever was being thrown.

"This used to be an open pit here; the guys would finish with the bones they'd stripped of meat and then throw them down to the truck below. And yes, they made a game out of it most of the time." We continued on until we came to a long room with large, shiny metal boxes encasing conveyor belts and cutting machines. Glazed yellow tile covered the walls.

Darrin asked me what I sensed there. I walked slowly into the room while the others stayed back at the door. At the far end of the room, beside the tallest metal box, which was just about shoulder height, I felt a sense of anger—and of something being thrown again. There was a knife lying on top of the tall metal case. Darrin walked over as soon as I pointed out where I felt all this emotion.

"This is right where the latest incident took place, and it scared us all pretty badly," Darrin said.

Darrin explained that the two men who worked in this area were at their stations, one on each end of the room. The guy on my side of the room was at the conveyor belt, and Darrin pointed to the flat surface of the tall, shiny metal case where the knife lay, then down to where the man stood beside it. The other man was across the room talking to Darrin's brother and uncle. Darrin had just walked in that day and was headed toward his brother and uncle at the far end of the room. Suddenly he heard something hit the wall behind him and clatter to the floor. Darrin had turned around to see the worker behind him backing up, white-faced. The worker started yelling, "The knife! Something threw the knife against the wall. I watched it take off from a dead stop!"

Darrin told me there was no slanted surface nor anything that could've allowed the knife to slide or move suddenly. Darrin had glanced over at the guys on the other end of the room and noted the look on his uncle's face, which told him right away something strange had happened. Darrin then explained that his uncle is a total skeptic. He doesn't believe in any type of paranormal shenanigans. When Darrin finally walked over to his uncle that day, he leaned in and whispered to Darrin, "I saw the knife take off and hit the wall too." Darrin's uncle was as shaken as the workers.

A sharp knife hurtling across a room would seem to be a seriously aggressive act to most people. It would definitely be cause for concern. Darrin and I talked a little while about that room, but the entire incident somehow still felt like a prank to me. More like maybe the little boy, Ray, was trying to get their attention.

Darrin explained that this knife incident is what really got him interested in ghost hunting. He'd already been going to Sherri's haunted-venue events, and this prompted him to get more involved. Darrin went right out and bought a digital voice recorder and soon after started the Amish Paranormal Society. He went right back to that room in the factory the night he bought the recorder, and that's when he got his first EVP. Darrin pulled out his voice recorder as we walked out of the room. He turned it on and I listened to the playback. Darrin could be heard saying, "You can throw that knife again if you want—just not at us." Then a voice clearly whispers, "*Where is it?*"

Darrin had caught a class A EVP for sure. And it sounded like a young boy's voice. Maybe it *was* Ray, the boy who'd drowned, just trying to let them know he was still there, that *he'd* thrown the knife, but more likely to get attention than for evil intent.

Next, Darrin led the way down a flight of stairs, pointing out a set of upper smoking alcoves, where he described an encounter he had one night.

He had been cleaning, washing down these alcoves, which got dirty after smoking the meat. They were made of glazed tile. Darrin explained that when they were clean, they reflected images very well, especially when anyone walked through the room. There was only one other guy there with Darrin that night, and he was somewhere else in the building. As Darrin washed down the tile, he could clearly see a person coming up behind him in the tile's reflection. The man asked, "How much longer until you're done?" Darrin answered that it shouldn't be too long, that he was on the last one. Just then, Darrin's coworker yelled from the other room: "Who are you talking to?" When his coworker walked in, Darrin realized he'd been having a conversation with "something," but it sure wasn't his coworker! Darrin asked his coworker if he'd just been talking, and he told Darrin he'd been out front but had heard Darrin carrying on a conversation with someone! That freaked Darrin out pretty badly too.

Not only a full-bodied apparition casting a shadow on the tiles, but an intelligent haunting, one that conversed with Darrin—it was the holy grail of ghost hunting. But then again, the family business had been run by Darrin's family members and ancestors for over a hundred years.

Another time, during their busy season, which is in November and December, Darrin had already worked a thirteen-hour day. He'd gone home, but needed to run back to the factory for something. He was there alone, and as he finished and walked to the door to leave, he heard someone whistling a tune! Darrin stopped and told them, "I've had a long day, but it you want to communicate with me, I'd be more than happy to stay a little while longer." Then he added, "I like to whistle too." Then Darrin whistled a little bit. Darrin waited, but nothing else happened so he turned to leave. Just then, something whistled again! Darrin waited a few minutes more and said, "Okay, I have to go now, but I'll be back in the morning." And as he turned to go, there was one quick, short whistle.

I asked Darrin if there had been any workers who liked to whistle, and he told me his prankster uncle had.

I told Darrin how cool I thought it was that his family business still had his family there in the afterlife! But I regretted expressing that sentiment soon after.

We descended the stairs into a small narrow room: the smoker, where the wood was burned and tended by whichever man was in charge. As soon as I walked into the room, a heavy, almost overwhelming sense of despair seemed to squash the life out of me. It was so severe, I suddenly had a lot of trouble getting my breath. I told Darrin what I was feeling, but he didn't respond. Walking toward the far end of the room, I came to the place where it was strongest.

"So much heaviness—sadness and despair, right here." I pointed at a small table and chair against the wall. "Someone in desperate pain—the negative energy is still here—the black thoughts, running over and over in someone's head; anguish, sorrow—helplessness to fight it, or overcome it." I tried to take in a deep breath through the feeling. It was a sensation like someone sitting squarely on my chest. I could barely breathe. Suddenly, the name "Earl" was whispered in my mind. "Who is Earl? I'm being told Earl?" *Was Earl enough? Was Earl okay? Did he do enough to help you?* I did not understand, and hoped Darrin would have some idea what it meant.

Darrin finally confessed that this made sense to him because his father had committed suicide. The room that they called the smoker is where his father worked most of the time. My own father had ended his life, and I could relate to the kind of pain this left behind in a family. Darrin's father must've sat here day after day, contemplating suicide, and this is what I had been sensing. It was just so sad there, so oppressive and thick with negative energy. I knew I needed to do something to try somehow to lighten things.

Darrin spoke again. "Earl is the man who stepped up and became like a father to me after my dad died. Earl saw me through everything, and he still thinks of me as his son."

I asked Darrin if he minded if I tried to talk to his dad. I was suddenly feeling a deep sense of guilt in the atmosphere, of a father's anguish that he'd left his young son, Darrin, and his family behind. And that, most of all, he regretted it.

Darrin gave me permission to try.

I sat down on a little stool beside the table. "Your family doesn't blame you; they love you and they understand." I paused, and hoped someone was listening. "Earl stepped up and was there for Darrin after you died," I told the quiet room. "Earl filled in for you; there's no reason to carry this pain and guilt any longer. Darrin turned out fine. He's a man now. He's running your business and doing very well. And he's happy. He doesn't blame you. He forgives you. It's time to go to God, to the light, to leave here and be happy now. You've suffered long enough."

Darrin and my friend Brian were standing a few feet away from me, and at that moment, they felt a cold breeze rush between them. They looked at one another, startled, and Darrin asked if Brian had felt that. Brian nodded. I stood up, and we all walked to the door.

It immediately felt better in the previously thick, depressing room. I couldn't believe how the atmosphere had changed, although I'd witnessed this before. The heaviness was completely gone, and even those without any psychic abilities could sense it.

We stood by the door talking quietly about the factory and what we'd seen and experienced so far. At one point, I mentioned one of the rooms being dead quiet, then I joked, "no pun intended." We headed back upstairs, comforted at what seemed to be a successful release of negative energy. The thought of possibly having reassured the spirit of Darrin's father and setting him free cast a warm glow upon us all. We wound up our brief investigation and said our goodbyes, and Darrin gave me a ring of my favorite Trail Bologna on my way out.

The next day, Darrin called and played an EVP. It was recorded while I'd been talking with the group, right after I'd spoken out loud to Darrin's dad. When I said, "It was dead quiet—no pun intended," there was an EVP of a little giggle, an invisible someone laughing at my joke! Once again, it sounded like a younger child.

I think Darrin's father's energy was released from that sad room, but I think that Ray, the young boy who drowned, stays on. Because he likes it there! It's his family, it's all he's ever known, and I don't think it will be easy convincing him to go to the light. To Ray, I believe the bologna factory is his *own* little slice of heaven. And Darrin is okay with that too.

———

I spoke with Darrin recently, and he told me that the week before, there had been several incidents that took place at the factory.

His twelve-year-old nephew, Jerrod, had been coming in occasionally with Darrin's brother. Jerrod and Darrin were the only ones in a particular section of the building that day. Darrin saw his nephew walk through the doorway to the other room, but then turn around suddenly and come back to where Darrin was. Darrin looked up and saw his nephew's face was ashy white. Darrin asked him what was wrong, but he just answered that nothing was. Darrin told his nephew he knew something was wrong just from the look on his face! Darrin walked over to him and noticed the hair on his arms was standing straight up. "You saw something didn't you?" Darrin asked him. Finally, he got it out of him. His nephew said he'd walked into the big room—the room where I'd sensed the bones being thrown—and saw a man with an apron walk from one side of the room, all the way across, and then disappear into the wall. It scared the poor kid half to death.

There is an old medicine cabinet on one wall in that room as well, and just a few days before the full-bodied apparition appeared, Darrin and his nephew saw the cabinet open up, then close itself again. Darrin wasn't going to say anything when it first happened so as not to scare his nephew. After all, he was only twelve. But then Darrin noticed his nephew staring at the medicine cabinet, so he asked him if he'd seen that happen. He had. They got the heck out of there that night. It was just a little too active for their taste!

PART TWO
RETURNS FROM BEYOND

As long as humans have existed, there have been ghost stories. Many of these stories concern loved ones returning after their death to say farewell, to give a message, or in some cases, to warn of some impending danger. Many other spirits and hauntings seem to have no rhyme or reason; the motive has been lost over the passage of time. As investigators and fellow human beings, we owe those who come back after death our efforts to understand their messages. Even if they came back just to say goodbye, we can be thankful they were able to manage what must be a very difficult feat. If it wasn't so difficult to return, there would be far more ghost stories.

7

NEVER SAY GOODBYE

My son James had returned many times right after his death, but the visits had slowed down some. It seemed that he showed up sometimes when I talked out loud to him. I actually did that a lot—it was almost unconscious. And then I'd catch myself doing it and worry that I was disturbing his peace, somehow calling him back with my ongoing pain. But I didn't mean to do that in any negative way, it was more a matter of including him in my life. And it just made me feel better. It got me through another day. The loss of a child is very hard.

After the rough investigation where I found out about the poor woman's body stuffed down a well, I arrived home to my little dog Bo Bo greeting me at the back door enthusiastically. I realized I was so tired, I needed to lie down for a quick nap before I did anything else, mostly to try to lose the headache I'd developed after using psychic abilities intensely.

"Ah, James, I'm glad to be home," I said out loud as I stretched out on the bed. I fell into a deep sleep. I'd barely been asleep ten minutes when suddenly the sound of the chain lock on my bedroom door smacking hard against the wood jerked me up, wide awake. Such a familiar and distinctive sound; I'd heard it a thousand times. I thought at first that maybe it was my husband, but no one was there. I stared at the swinging chain and called, "James?" Nothing, no response.

So much for my nap. I got up and went in search of my husband, only to find him in the basement studio. I told him what had happened, and we sat there for a while in silence, each lost in our own thoughts. Finally, I went back upstairs to get that cup of tea I'd been craving all evening.

Later that night when I went to bed, I was almost asleep when something tapped twice—hard—on my mattress. I jumped, and once again spoke out loud. "James, if that's you, I hear you. I felt that. I love you." The ongoing visits from him left me mystified. Yes, they'd slowed down some, but they were still happening. I wanted to believe he was okay, that he just popped in sometimes, especially when I forgot and spoke out loud to him. I was really trying to break that habit.

———

Sometimes, those closest to us can lead us to what we didn't expect to find. My husband's niece Tanya had somehow pulled through a devastating stroke a couple months before. It had been touch and go for a while, with the doctors saying she would not live. Then they revised their prognosis to say that if she did, she would be a vegetable, unable to ever lead a normal life, destined to be institutionalized forever.

After the shock began to fade—at this relatively young woman being at death's door—the praying started. And then, day by day, Tanya began to improve. We were unable to get away to see her immediately after her stroke, but we stayed in contact with family on her progress.

My husband's family had always been fairly devout; they always said grace before our meals at yearly gatherings, and they lived their Christian values. These were good and decent people who not only talked the talk, but walked the walk. They helped others whenever they could and were impressive both in their faith and their stoicism.

Finally, over a long holiday weekend, we drove the several hours to see Tanya after she'd been transferred to a rehab center. There were both tears and smiles. Tanya had retained her sense of humor, joking about the helmet they made her wear while her missing piece of skull remained covered only by a flap of skin. I couldn't help but remember that my son had this same surgery and didn't survive it. Tanya still tired easily, so after a half-hour visit, we made our way to my sister-in-law's house for a bite to eat before the trip home. We were anxious to hear more about everything that had taken place. Tanya's husband, Dwayne, usually a very quiet, amiable guy, had a lot to say that day.

"Tanya told me her dad sent her back," Dwayne began. Puzzled, I waited to hear him out, as Tanya's dad, Gerald, had been dead for almost a decade. Dwayne shook his head, seemingly still amazed, then gazed steadily at me. "And Tanya said her dead aunt was there too."

Dumbfounded, I asked what had happened.

After Tanya had awakened from her stroke and surgery, she told Dwayne that her dad and her aunt had walked up to her. They told her it wasn't her time yet, and she had to go back! She told this to Dwayne as soon as she woke up.

I explained to Dwayne that I was writing a book about just these kinds of things.

"That's not all that's happened," said my husband's sister. "Did you know that Dwayne saw something in the weeks before Gerald died? And on the night he died too?"

We told her that we hadn't heard about this, and Dwayne, who never said much even on a talkative day, began to tell us the story.

"Gerald had been in the hospital and had descended into a coma. No one could wake him up, and they knew if he didn't wake soon, things must be moving toward his end. They'd all tried talking to Gerald, telling him to get up, doing their best to rouse him. One day, I was sitting in Gerald's room with him, when I looked up to see what looked like a window appear in the wall, with people moving behind it. There hadn't been a window there before! Suddenly, a woman stepped right out of the wall. She walked to Gerald's bed, took his hand, and said 'Wake up.' As soon as she touched his hand, Gerald sat up! He was wide awake. 'Mommy,' Gerald said, and then the woman just disappeared. Then Gerald looked over and saw me there, and began thanking me for all I'd done for his family and for him."

My sister-in-law chimed in. "When I came into Gerald's hospital room, Dwayne told me what had happened, and then he described the woman who came. It was Gerald's mother—to a T—and Dwayne had never met her. She'd died long before Tanya and Dwayne got married."

I was speechless after hearing this incredible story. I knew and trusted these people; they'd never make something like this up. My sister-in-law then began another story.

The night her husband, Gerald, died, Dwayne was sitting there beside his bed, and my sister-in-law noticed that Dwayne kept looking up at the ceiling. She said Dwayne was acting very strange and just kept glancing up at one spot.

Dwayne looked slightly embarrassed, and softly said, "I thought maybe I was going crazy."

I asked him what he saw up near the ceiling.

"Jesus. I saw the face of Jesus. I think he came for Gerald."

The table fell silent. Far be it from me to discount this vision—I myself had seen too many unexplainable things. I'd also witnessed my son's returns after his death. So I quietly nodded. Dwayne looked uncomfortable.

I don't know what Dwayne saw, but knowing his honesty, I am not prepared to call him a liar. And like all Christians who hope that the Lord himself might come for us when it's our time, many of us can relate to this.

I now looked at quiet, unassuming Dwayne in a new way. I already knew he was a good husband, a great father, and a kind and decent man. But now I knew he'd been blessed with visions of things many of us may never get to see.

I drove home that day through a pouring rainstorm, deep in thought about God, life, death, and what awaits us afterward. All I discovered was that the more I learned, the less I knew.

———

The next day, I drove to meet a lady for a ghost-story interview. A light rain was falling as I made my way to my favorite coffee shop to meet an old friend I hadn't seen for a while. Maura, originally born in Ireland, and her husband, Dick, had been friends with my aunt and uncle, so I'd met them many years before. I also knew their daughter, who was an artist and came to my music performances occasionally. Dick had been a lifelong bluegrass musician, so he and I also had many musician friends in common. Maura's husband had passed away a few years before, but I'd heard through their daughter that Maura had some stories to tell me, and I definitely wanted to hear them.

I maneuvered my car into a parking space and pulled my hood up against the raindrops. It had been a cold, wet day. I ordered a cup of chai and sat down in the window alcove. Maura arrived moments later, smiling and carrying a bag that she laid on our table. "It's an answering machine," she told me mysteriously, as I gave her a quizzical look. But she just shook her head, not yet ready to tell me what it meant. Maura pulled out a chair and sat as I went to order coffee and scones. I carried her decaf and the blueberry scones to the table.

Maura's pleasant hazel eyes crinkled when she laughed, and her red hair and fair complexion proclaimed her Irish heritage. I was very curious about the answering machine, but politely made small talk as we sipped our hot drinks and nibbled the delicious bakery treats. Finally, I got down to business.

"I know you had some experiences after Dick died, and I'd like to hear everything."

Maura nodded and pointed to the answering machine she'd brought. "If you can hook this up, you can hear for yourself." Seeing my puzzled look again, she smiled.

Maura told me she had several stories to tell, and they were kind of intertwined, so she started from the beginning. The first thing she told me was that she and Dick had had a son who was killed in an accident.

I told her I was sorry and that I'd heard that from her daughter.

Maura nodded. "The night our son died, my husband Dick woke up at 2:00 a.m. gasping for breath and choking, unable to get air, and just as that was happening, the phone rang. But when I answered it, there was no one there." Maura frowned slightly at the memory. "Two hours later, the police came and told us that our son had died at 2:00 a.m.—the official cause was he'd choked to death." *Oh, how sad,* I thought.

Maura continued on.

She and Dick had discussed it afterward, wondering if somehow their son was able to call them when he died, trying to reach out one last time. And of course they wondered if somehow Dick had experienced what their son was going through—fighting for air and choking, which then woke Dick up. The more the couple talked about the phone call and how Dick couldn't breathe when he awoke, the more they felt it was their son trying to let them know.

Maura looked sad as she sipped her coffee. She continued with the rest of the story.

Dick began to have some health problems of his own. Dick's bluegrass band wasn't together at that time, and some of his friends wanted to hire Dick's band for an event. So Dick told them about a good band that they could hire instead. Maura and Dick decided to take their friends to see the band perform locally that night. They sat right up front. It was a loud nightclub setting, and while they were all watching the band, Dick's head fell onto Maura's shoulder. She thought he was just fooling around with her, as he often did. But when Maura asked him what he was doing, she saw that his eyes were rolled back.

Maura screamed and the band onstage noticed immediately and asked if there were any EMTs in the house. There were, and they came running. Dick's heart had stopped—he was clinically dead. Maura said it seemed like forever until the ambulance arrived. Finally when it did, the paramedics used the paddles on Dick, and his heart restarted. But it had been at least seventeen minutes since his heart stopped.

At the hospital, they did a procedure for blocked arteries, but because Dick had been dead for so long, the surgeon didn't think he would ever wake up. And yet, somehow he did. It took Dick a little while to come back to his old self, but one day the surgeon came in to talk to him. He told Dick he'd never had a patient die for so long, and the surgeon wanted to know if Dick had seen the light. Dick said no, but that he'd been trying to catch a little cherub angel he'd been following. Dick said it was just wonderful where he was, that he felt love and joy, and the pain he'd suffered for years since he'd had spinal surgery was gone— at least until he slammed back into his body.

This event really changed Dick too. Ever since their son had died, Dick couldn't stand to go to funerals. But after Dick himself died that day, he didn't feel this way any longer. In fact, he would often go to funerals just to talk to the survivors and reassure them how wonderful it was on the other side!

I told Maura that maybe that's why he didn't *go* at that time—because he was needed here to tell others about his experience.

Maura nodded again and told me she'd wondered the same thing.

"So what is the answering machine for?" I finally asked her, and Maura smiled again.

"That's the most amazing part of all," Maura said.

After a few more years together, Dick had been diagnosed with cancer. He lived with it for over a year, and he and Maura had a lot of talks—about their son, about Dick's experience with death, and toward the end, Dick promised Maura he'd try to come back to her if he could.

Maura and Dick's granddaughter's birthday was three weeks after Dick died. The girl had been having a terrible time because she and her grandpa had always been so close, going to breakfast each Sunday and spending lots of time together. The granddaughter was taking his death really hard. On the girl's birthday, Maura came home from the store and saw the light on the answering machine blinking, showing that a message had come in. And when Maura played it back, she sat in shock. The message was an eerie voice saying "Hello"—it had a very hollow, scratchy, echoey tone to it. But even so, Maura could hear that it was her dead husband, Dick. She called her daughter and everyone she could think of, and they all came over and agreed—it was definitely Dick. There was no number on the caller ID—it really was a call from the grave.

Maura and I sat in silence for a few minutes after she relayed her story.

Then Maura told me her daughter also had an experience if I wanted to hear about it. I told her I did.

Right before Maura and Dick's son died, their daughter, the boy's sister, went to an antique shop one day and found a wooden rocker that she just fell in love with. She brought it home and used it regularly. Her best friend and neighbor was there one day with her young son, and he had wandered into the room where the chair was kept. The boy called to Maura's daughter from the other room, "Did you know your new chair says 'Believe' on it?"

Maura's daughter was puzzled and didn't understand what the boy meant at first—because the chair didn't have anything written on it. So Maura's daughter brought the chair out into the light, and sure enough, the word "Believe" was spelled out across the back of it, seemingly written in the grain of the wood! A week later, Maura and Dick's son—her brother—was killed. It spooked Maura's daughter so badly that she covered the chair up with a sheet and couldn't bear to have it in the house. She gave it to her neighbor's son. By that time, it no longer said "Believe" on it. The word went away on its own somehow, just as mysteriously as it had appeared.

Maura looked thoughtful, and then began to tell me another story about their son's return.

That wasn't the only time Maura's daughter believes her brother came back to her after his death. Maura's daughter is an artist and had been in a real rut, artistically speaking. Just burnt out and unable to think of anything new to draw or paint. She had already done a painted dinnerware line for several large chain stores. But she found herself in a stagnant state of mind. Her brother had been her biggest supporter, often watching over her shoulder as she painted. So obviously the girl was devastated when her brother died. Not long afterwards, while she was going through her painter's block, she had a dream. Her brother came up behind her in the dream and grabbed her shoulder. Then he whispered in her ear: "Try watercolors."

Maura's daughter had never tried watercolors, although Maura had bought her daughter a set long before. The daughter kept them stored in a closet, unused. When she woke up the next morning after the dream, she came down to her studio, and in the middle of the floor sat a small tube of red watercolor paint. There was no way it could've been dropped there—her only watercolors were in the old set stored in the closet, which was nowhere near her studio area. Maura's daughter knew then that her brother had come back to her in her time of need. Somehow, he left the tube of watercolors to reinforce what he'd told his sister in the dream. As her biggest fan, he'd always helped and encouraged her before. And he helped her after death too. It worked. Maura's daughter went on to create new and successful lines in watercolor.

I told Maura I thought it was great that a loving brother was seemingly still showing his sister support. That had to make them both feel good.

We finished our scones and coffee and said our good-byes. Maura asked me to take the answering machine so I could hear and record Dick's call from beyond the grave. And I did. You can hear this and see other evidence at my Facebook author page, www.facebook.com/debrarobinsonauthor. I only wish my son James could have called and left me the sound of *his* voice.

———

Later that night I was sitting in my usual spot on the sofa, laptop on my knees and feet up on the coffee table in front of me. I was home alone with just the dogs. My little dog Bo Bo was curled up beside me on the couch in his usual spot. And James's big Lab, Leia, was asleep in the kitchen. The door to the kitchen, about three feet away on my right, was closed. This is the same door that James had scratched his initials into one night after he died. I had the TV on mute, so the room was quiet and still. Suddenly I heard—*click*. The sound of the old metal doorknob turning made me jump. With a metallic rattle and a click, the door slowly swung open. From my position on the sofa I could see Leia fast asleep a few feet inside the door on a rug. So it wasn't her up against it.

"James, is that you?" I always talked to him when these things happened, just in case he wanted me to, just in case he needed the acknowledgement. But there was no other sound. I got up to check the door in case there was anything else written on it this time, but there was nothing different. James's initials were still scratched into the century-old wood—they'd somehow appeared one night right after he died, after I'd heard the sound of scratching and then five knocks, apparently to get my attention. I looked down at James's old dog, almost sixteen and very frail now, still snoring, fast asleep on the rug. I sighed and closed the door again. I went back to my work. A short time after this happened, James's old friend Tazz posted on Facebook.

"My computer just opened and turned itself on!" I quizzed him about it, thinking maybe he opened it himself and forgot, after maybe having a few beers or something. But Tazz was stone-cold sober.

He told me he'd gone to bed and looked over at his computer, thinking maybe he'd use it before he went to sleep. It was closed tight. Then when he couldn't sleep, he decided to get up and go online, and the computer was wide open and turned on! I told him what had just happened here.

Tazz and I both knew that James had visited him before. Just after James had died, he'd manifested as a blue light hovering over Tazz that had scared poor Tazz's friends half to death when they witnessed it! I finally had more peace about these things. I didn't feel James's pain or desperation any longer, and I hoped it was just his way of letting us know he was still around and just visiting us all occasionally.

————

The next day was finally the first beautiful one in what was turning out to be a very late spring. It had been cold and snowy far into March and April that year. I'd spent a few hours cleaning up the yard, picking up sticks, and raking leaves. When I headed into the house to get a cup of tea, it was almost dark. My husband had been in the basement studio working, and as I checked my email in the living room, he passed by, headed outside with the clippers. He'd wanted to help me do some yard work but had lost track of time.

"There's just enough light to cut the ornamental grasses back," he said on his way past the doorway.

"Okay," I mumbled, only half-listening, preoccupied with answering some emails. I heard him come back ten minutes later, having cut back all three plantings of our tall grasses.

He sat down at his laptop in the other room. "Where are my glasses?" he asked. After I told him I hadn't seen them, I heard him go off searching for them in the basement. But he was soon back upstairs. "Oh no, I must've lost them out back somewhere. I'll never find them in the dark." He usually wore them hooked into the neck of his T-shirt.

My husband walked out back and over toward the first clump of grass he'd cut. As he bent over, peering into the dark at the thick, golden stubble, he heard someone call, "Dad?" from the fire pit area at the opposite end of the yard. He turned, confused, thinking maybe I'd come out, but then realized it was James's voice he'd heard! He walked across the yard to the pit, where he'd dumped all the grass cuttings. Puzzled, he stood in the dark beside it, gazing around for the origin of the voice. Suddenly, he spotted a tiny glint from the fire pit—it was the stem of his glasses sticking up from the mass of long fronds. He pulled the glasses out, knowing he never would have seen them if James's voice had not drawn him there.

"Thanks, James," he told him, smiling.

My husband came back inside and told me what happened. I believe James stopped by just in time to lend some help. If he hadn't, the glasses would've settled into the brush and been burnt up at our next fire. James seems to have found ways of helping us out from time to time.

The next night, I believe James locked the basement door. I hadn't been down there for a while, and my husband claimed he hadn't locked it. It's a very old sliding chain lock, probably original to the house, a 1917 version. The only reason I could think of that James might do this was that I'd had an accident not long before—I'd fallen down our second-floor stairs and broken my leg that previous winter. Maybe James was trying to keep me away from the basement steps, just in case! He'd always teased me about my absentminded-professor ways. Just the night before, my husband came in complaining again.

"Did you lock the basement door? I sure didn't!"

"No, I haven't been anywhere near it."

"Well, it couldn't do it by itself!"

Maybe it could. I believe James is still here, trying to help us out. He knows he was all we had, our only child, and he always promised to take care of us. Maybe he still keeps his promise.

8

MESSAGES

My old friend Sarah was a former waitress at one of my music venues, and we shared a lot of history, psychically speaking. Much of our haunted history is told in my first book, which recounts Sarah's series of tragedies, including the death of her fiancé. Then she experienced the ghostly returns of her loved one. Sarah remains a very good friend to this day. To make a long story short, as I read her palm after we first met, I could tell she was pregnant—before she knew it herself—and being able to reveal this unknown pregnancy, which Sarah swore wasn't true, prompted Sarah to hire me for a psychic party at her house. This is where I come to someone's home to do group readings for their friends.

As I prepared for Sarah's party, while doing the preliminary clairvoyant readings I usually do, I was suddenly given a vision of a lump on her fiancé's testicle. It was confusing and potentially embarrassing to me, as these were very young people in their early twenties. As it turned out, her fiancé, Evan, who was the father of her son, had already been to several doctors about this lump. Each doctor had told him it was harmless, but I wasn't so sure. Mostly because I believe that when I'm shown these things, it's for a reason, and it means something important—often it's like a warning. Later on, Evan became ill, but before anyone could find out exactly why, he was killed in an automobile wreck. But as these things sometimes go, I wasn't shown *this* wreck, unfortunately.

Sarah and I stayed in touch on and off over those several years after Evan died. Then one day Sarah called me, having decided to have another group get-together for her friends. We chatted a little and then set up her reading party. Sarah gave me each of her friends' first names.

Before each party I like to do preliminary clairvoyant readings to try to tailor my reading to what each person needs. My clairvoyance has always manifested itself as a light that comes from all directions when I close my eyes, usually forming pictures or words. I've been shown everything from diseased organs to engagement rings. It sounds strange, but this is how it's always worked for me. So I closed my eyes to see what the light formed for each name. When I came to one name on the list, Brea, the light formed the word "cancer"—and I wrote it down. But I really thought it must mean Brea's horoscope sign because they were all young women in their twenties. I had learned early on not to try to interpret too deeply what I was shown—that the interpretation was always best done by the person getting the reading.

The day of the reading party, Sarah and her friends met me at Uncorked, the haunted wine bar owned by my friends Joe and Lorrie. They've always graciously allowed me to use their beautiful and private back room to do readings. When Sarah came in that day, she told me Brea couldn't make it for her reading. I thought about giving the paper with Brea's reading on it to Sarah to take to her. But since I thought I might see Brea when she rescheduled her reading, I tucked it away instead and promptly forgot all about it.

A couple more years went by, and I ran into Sarah again one night. As we caught up on things, Sarah told me some sad news about her best friend Brea; she'd been diagnosed with breast cancer and was in the fight of her life. At her young age, it was a rare and particularly aggressive form. By then, I'd forgotten about the earlier reading I'd tucked away. I got a nagging feeling of déjà vu, and the more I thought about it, I finally remembered the reading. I felt terribly guilty. Perhaps this could've somehow been averted if only she'd shown up as scheduled or if only I'd have given her written reading to Sarah.

Not long afterward, I saw Brea in a restaurant where I played music. She was a beautiful young woman, who'd had striking, nearly white-blond hair and a pretty face. We talked and I did my best to encourage her. She had a positive outlook and was ready to fight the breast cancer. By then, she had a scarf on to cover the loss of her hair due to chemo. My heart went out to her, so young, so brave.

Sarah kept me informed on Facebook as Brea fought her desperate battle. The posts were sad, and eventually, after a long, hard struggle, Brea passed away, surrounded by her family. After she died, Brea's mother emailed me, and I tried to offer her what comfort I could—although I knew from losing my own son just how difficult those first few months are for a parent. Brea's mother was devastated.

I explained to Brea's mom what to watch for to know if Brea was returning to her—odd sounds, lights flashing, TV problems, crackling noises, as if electricity was sparking or paper or a plastic water bottle was being crumpled. But Brea's mother Shelly hadn't heard any of these things. I explained that sometimes people don't come back at all after their deaths—they go straight to the light and are at peace. This is especially true when they know their end is coming and can make peace with it, as Brea had probably done.

A few more months went by. Finally Brea's mother emailed me again, desperate to hear from her daughter. I could feel the pain in her email. The devastation of losing your child is like no other agony on earth. Out of compassion, I told her I would try to see something about her daughter. Though, due to the inconsistent nature of psychic abilities and mediumship in general, I was afraid to get her hopes up. Plus, Brea's mother was in so much pain, I wanted to tread very carefully so as not to cause her any more.

After I finished her email, I sat back on my sofa and closed my eyes. And I saw…bubbles…then these bubbles began morphing into balloons! This seemed inconsequential, even silly, and meant nothing to me, but I thought there was some small chance it meant something to Brea's mom. I sat for a few minutes, deciding whether or not to even say anything—and finally decided I should. I emailed her to tell her what I saw. She was ecstatic. Then she explained what it meant.

"Right before Brea died, I asked her to please come back and give me a sign if she could, something that only I would know. And Brea agreed to try to do this. I think this is the sign I wanted, because no one else knows this." Unbeknownst to me, or to any of Brea's close friends such as Sarah, Brea had a nickname in college, before she moved to the area. Her college name was Bubbelz.

"Brea also worked in the entertainment division of a basket company, making balloon animals for children who visited during school field trips and other events," Brea's mom said. She believed Brea had given me this sign specifically for her, fulfilling what she'd asked Brea to do.

When I spoke to Sarah, who had never heard about Brea's nickname or her job with balloons, she was simply thrilled. Both Sarah and Brea's mom felt that this information was proof Brea had survived after death. Brea's mom then told me she was making a trip to our area soon and would like to meet with me. I knew she wanted more information from Brea. I told Sarah of my reluctance to meet Brea's mom, mostly because I couldn't guarantee anything would come through psychically from Brea. But I also knew her pain, so I wanted to help. I also know it's not up to me what comes through from the other side, which is one of the sadder and more frustrating aspects of having a psychic gift.

Sarah emailed me a couple months later that Shelly, Brea's mother, was in town and wanted to get together for lunch, and possibly a reading, the next day. We decided to meet at a beautiful winery and restaurant halfway between Sarah's town and mine.

The drive down was gorgeous—by May, spring had finally arrived in Ohio. Sarah and Shelly met me in the parking lot outside the building and we made small talk as we walked inside and were seated. We were the only ones there.

While driving down, I'd felt Brea was trying to show me something. Finally, when I closed my eyes at a red light, I realized it was a starfish. I didn't know what this might mean, but I knew I needed to bring this up to Brea's mother. I also wanted to tell Shelly the cancer story with

Sarah there to confirm it, even though I was ashamed I hadn't followed through.

We ordered our lunch and as they brought the salads, we began to talk. I still felt ill at ease, mostly because I was worried about Shelly's feelings and about the grief I knew she still carried for her daughter. I didn't want to make it any worse. But my fears were short-lived, as Shelly wanted to talk. I could relate as I'd felt the same way right after my son's death.

Shelly believed Brea had come back to her since she'd died. The first time it was something that Brea always did—every time they were ready to go anywhere, if she was behind Shelly, Brea would notice if her mom's hair was messed up and flick it, telling her it needed to be fixed in the back. This usually happened from Shelly having lain down on it. Brea would flick her hair and laugh, and then would always comb it for her mother. Right after Brea died, Shelly walked into the room where Brea had stayed at the end of her life. Shelly had just entered the room, when she felt someone flick the back of her hair. The window wasn't open, the fan wasn't on, and there was nothing else that could've caused it. I understood completely, as something similar had happened—and continues to happen—with my son James as well, and I told her about it.

James used to walk past the sofa—which is at a right angle to the wall so that you can cross behind it—and pat me on the head. I can't tell you how many times I've felt that gentle pat on my head since he's died. Just out of the blue, when I'm least thinking about it! My husband has felt the same thing. It was just something James did when he was alive, a lot, to both of us. We think he still does this when he stops by occasionally. It actually comforts me.

Shelly thought Brea was doing the same thing. She mentioned something else that had happened recently. Shelly was going to a flea market that Brea just loved. They'd always gone there together. Usually Shelly and her daughter arrived at the crack of dawn when no one else was around. After Brea died, Shelly searched for things to do to distract herself. So she decided to go to the flea market. Shelly went just as early as she and Brea always had, and her daughter was on her mind as she pulled up and got out. She'd just stepped out of the car, when her cell phone went off—with Brea's ring—the sound of a doorbell. It sounded twice! There was no one else around anywhere. And no one else Shelly knows has Brea's ringtone. Of course Shelly checked her phone, but it didn't show any number calling. My friend Sarah also got a charge hearing about these visitations. Sarah really missed Brea too.

"Brea was just letting you know she was there with you, in spirit," I told Shelly, and Shelly smiled. I knew it wasn't much comfort, but at least it was a little.

Sarah chimed in with her own story. Right after her fiancé, Evan, was killed, Sarah was sitting alone at the table and felt a hand go up the back of her neck and into her hair, then the hand began rubbing around on her scalp. Sarah screamed and totally freaked out.

I asked Sarah if she spoke out loud to Evan when this happened.

"No, and now I feel bad that I didn't put it together. But at the time I was really upset by it—an invisible hand on my neck and hair! Evan had died about two hours before this happened."

I thought maybe this was as good a time as any to tell Brea's mom about the info I'd gotten for her daughter all those years ago. I felt pretty awful about it because it might have made the difference between Brea's life and death. I told Shelly about the reading I did for her daughter—the reading that she missed. I explained how then I forgot all about it until it was too late.

After I told her the cancer story, Sarah added a few things that I'd forgotten; that I'd told Brea there was something about twins. Sarah said that she and Brea had a good laugh over that later on. She wasn't ready for more babies! After she got the breast cancer though, Sarah remembered this, and wondered if *that's* what twins meant, her breasts. I think it did.

I told her I'd forgotten that part and that I only wished I'd have seen things more clearly or paid more attention to what it might mean. I was almost ashamed to look at Shelly. But Shelly didn't blame me. I decided to tell her then about the starfish I'd seen on my way down, just to see if it rang any bells. Turns out, she knew exactly what it referred to.

"Yes, it does mean something! One time we went on vacation to the beach and I found a starfish. It was so adorable, just this tiny, living, star-shaped creature, and I wanted to take it home with us. Brea was very upset with me; she didn't want me to take it, and of course she was right because it soon died. She was so angry with me over it, I don't know if she ever forgave me for that."

I think Brea was trying to give her mom and her friend Sarah a message by sending me a picture of that starfish before I met them for lunch. And I think she was trying to say that life is fragile and that beautiful things die sometimes—when we interfere, and sometimes even when we don't. And above all, I think she used that starfish to show her mom she'd forgiven her for any of the silly things in their past.

I was filled with wonder at the strange stories I'd heard so far and what lengths our loved ones go to just to let us know they still exist after death. My dad had snapped his fingers in my face only hours after we'd found he'd committed suicide. I told Shelly and Sarah about the phone call from Maura's husband from the grave, how he was somehow able to say hello, and then Sarah's face froze—she said the same thing had happened to her.

It had been with a friend of hers. Sarah had a close friend who was killed; in fact, he was shot. Sarah came home from work one day and saw her answering machine was blinking, so she played it back. There was a whisper recorded on it, but it was real fast, and she couldn't make it out. She played it again several times, but still couldn't understand it. Sarah's boyfriend was sleeping at the time, and she needed to be quiet, so she waited until he went to work and could turn it up really loud. Sarah called Tess, the sister of the guy who was killed, hoping that she could help decipher the message—Sarah just felt deep inside that it was from Tess's brother! Knowing Sarah as I do, her loyalty as a friend has always been admirable.

Sarah knew the boy who'd been shot was very close to his sister, Tess. They were very much best friends. The brother and sister ran around together, teased, and one-upped each other constantly. Tess finally arrived at Sarah's house, and together, the two deciphered the message. It was from Tess's brother, who'd been shot and killed—it said, "Find Tess, tell her there's something I know now." Tess was completely freaked out! She knew this message was from her brother, and she knew he was still one-upping her from beyond the grave. Her brother was rubbing in the fact that he was in the afterlife and letting her know he knew more about it than his sister did. Not too long after that, Sarah played his answering machine message for the boy's other sister, and *she* threw the machine across the room! Sarah yelled at her not to break it because she wanted to save it. Sarah still has it stored in her basement. It was the most amazing thing for Sarah and Tess to get this proof from beyond.

Sarah, Brea's mom, and I talked a little longer, then paid our checks and said goodbye.

A few weeks later when my book was released, I drove to meet Sarah again for lunch and deliver a copy to her. Turns out, she thought she'd had a visit the night before from Evan, her former fiancé and her son's father.

Sarah was lying in bed and heard a crackling sound, like a water bottle being squeezed. She opened her eyes and listened, and then decided to ignore it. Then her little boy, who was lying beside her napping, sat up. Sarah asked him what was wrong, and he said, "Didn't you hear that crackling noise, Mom?" Sarah told him she thought she had, but that it was probably nothing and to go back to sleep.

I told Sarah it was probably Evan—that's the same noise James made when he came back. It's very like an electric sparking sound, like papers being crinkled or a water bottle crackling when you squeeze it.

"That describes it perfectly. I think he just came back to see us, because we were both lying on the bed napping." Sarah looked wistful, and shook her head. "We miss him."

For one so young, Sarah has been through so much.

I think that our loved ones do whatever they can to let us know they're still here with us. But sometimes, the same can be said for spirits we *don't* know too. Sarah told me about a ghost she saw one night in her house. It scared her, yet the apparition didn't really feel threatening. She was lying in bed with her little boy asleep next to her. He crawled into bed with her a lot. She was looking into the hallway and saw a tall man walk by. He took two steps through the hall, with his head down, as though he was sad. Sarah couldn't see any features or clothes, just a solid white shape, but she could tell it was a man.

Sarah's young son is six and still terrified to sleep in his room because of the ongoing haunting in their house. This is the same house where Sarah innocently invited a ghost hunter one night to record EVPs after hearing sounds, in hopes that it was Evan coming back to them. The EVP recorded growls and an evil voice saying, "Sarah, you're dead." Her son always sees a black shadow in his room, which is why he won't sleep there anymore. One night, the boy awoke to see a woman hovering over him, and he tried to wake his mom but he couldn't get her to wake up. He was really terrified, and even more so by the fact that his mom couldn't seem to be awakened to save him.

A friend of Sarah's saw this same shadow go into the closet one night. He said it moved really quickly. He went over to the closet, looked through it all, and nothing was there. Sarah used to see it all the time too. She feels the greatest sense of a presence in their basement—that's where the investigator picked up the EVPs of the growling and the threatening voice.

After our lunch, I drove home. Brea's, my son's, and Sarah's friends' returns were on my mind the entire way. I remembered another recent mysterious visitation I'd witnessed—I'd even helped deliver a message because of it.

I'd just given a lecture a month before at a large county library on the Ancient Art and Science of Palmistry. It was well attended and things were going great. I'd presented three-fourths of the information and was nearing the end of my program. I use a very big poster of a palm with all of the lines represented and a laser pointer to explain the various meanings behind each line. Since I need to move quickly from one area of the palm to another to fit in all the information in one hour, I have to map out the lecture carefully. I reserve a question-and-answer period at the end, but really can't stop during the presentation to answer anything.

On this particular night, other than two cell phone calls being taken by attendees—which almost derailed my train of thought—it had been fairly uneventful. A few people asked for clarifications during the presentation, and luckily I was able to answer them without getting too far off track.

I was rounding the home stretch when a lady in front took advantage of a brief lull as I searched for the thought I wanted to convey.

"Can you do a reading for me right now?" she blurted out suddenly.

I stood, mouth open, trying to think of the best way to say, "Um, no—the other hundred people sitting behind you might be offended," without sounding rude! Instead, I politely explained that I needed to wrap up the lecture, and maybe I could speak with her afterward. But she wasn't having any of it.

"What do you see for me, right now?" she insisted. This was getting out of control. Plus it was inconveniencing everyone else. I honestly didn't know what to do other than stop everything and focus in on her for a moment. I stared at her face and heard the name "Harold" whispered inside my head. The rest of the crowd held their collective breath.

"I see someone named Harold around you, trying to come through. Do you know a Harold?"

The woman thought for a moment then shook her head. "No, I don't know any Harolds," she said. I tilted my head quizzically, listening again. "It's definitely Harold, or Harry," I said.

The woman again denied knowing anyone by that name. *Great, wires sure got crossed on that one!* I couldn't figure out why I was hearing that name so strongly, and I was confused. This was slightly embarrassing, but it happens sometimes.

I continued on as best I could, after explaining that sometimes I pick up things for others or that sometimes spirits seem to jump in for someone else and that it's hard to sort out exactly who it's meant for or what exactly it means from a psychic perspective. The woman quieted down after this.

I finished the lecture, took some questions, thanked the audience, and it was over. Many people in the crowd lined up to speak to me afterward, and finally one lady who'd been seated far in the back and had waited patiently for the line to move, reached me. She leaned across the lectern confidentially, as those around us waited their turn.

"You know that woman in front, the one who you saw Harold around?" I nodded. "She worked at the hospital, every day, with my husband. I don't know why she didn't tell you." I waited, not understanding.

"My husband died this past year. His name was Harold!" she said, a look of astonishment on her face.

"Oh, so that's what it meant!"

The woman nodded her head, perplexed. "I don't know why she didn't tell you she knew a Harold—she worked with him every single day!"

I realized then how hard Harold must've tried to get me to hear him, to try to get the woman in front to recognize him, for his wife's sake. Just so his wife would know he was there—his wife, who had sat too far back in the room and was too polite to blurt anything out! I told Harold's wife that this was probably Harold's way of letting her know he was there for her and that he was okay. She thanked me gratefully, then walked away. I still don't know why the woman in the front row didn't acknowledge her coworker that night. But I do know that sometimes people forget names of close friends or even family when put on the spot by a psychic. Harold was probably as frustrated about it as I was!

9

GIFTS FROM BEYOND

We held our annual charity event in James's honor at the end of August, and I was tired, but tired in a good way. It took about a week to recover from all the work it involved. The James Short Memorial Session had become huge since its modest beginnings just after James's death. This year was the biggest yet, and from noon until 11:00 p.m., pro rollerbladers, food, and music—James's favorite things—were combined into one event where everyone had a lot of fun. And the money the event raised helped many charities throughout the year as well.

We'd had houseguests all week. James's old friend from Detroit (who had encountered our home's ghost in his younger years on an overnight stay), his girlfriend, and two other old friends. One of the legends of the skating industry flew in from California to emcee the event. They'd all just left a few hours before, and I already missed them terribly. But I was also looking forward to relaxing and getting back to my routine.

I hadn't had enough time to myself to think while all the hoopla was going on, and now I wanted to rehash several things that had happened, things that again pointed to James being the culprit. First, I'd run into my next-door neighbor in the driveway between our houses, and after she asked if I was working on a follow-up to my first book, of course the topic of James came up.

"I've never told you before, I was kind of afraid to, but now that some time has passed, you should know." She hesitated and I told her it was okay, that I'd like to hear whatever it was.

"That week after James died, I swore I saw his beanie pacing up and down the driveway, back and forth, back and forth." Her kitchen window looked out on our driveway and her short stature only allowed her to see the tops of heads that walked past. James and his friends had done just that, many times, on the way to his childhood hangout, the "shed." James had moved back into the shed just months before he was killed.

"Then my husband cornered me," she continued. "He told me he thought he was going crazy 'cause he thought he saw Jamie several times out there. Once I told him I had too, we knew it was for real." The neighbors still often called him Jamie, his childhood nickname.

I thanked her for telling me, and shook my head sadly as I went back to my guests. There were no words.

Now that all my houseguests were gone, I wanted to get outside, breathe the night air, and gather my thoughts about my neighbor's revelation. I'd missed my nightly walks with my little dog Bo Bo each evening. I'd had to postpone taking them to tend to my guests.

I was coming down the front staircase for my walk, thinking about the odd occurrences during the previous busy week. I rounded the corner on the landing and started down the final flight, when right beside the wall covered with James's pictures, I ran into a huge bug—I thought.

"Aaahhhh," I shrieked, as the heavy sound of a large bug's rapidly vibrating wings buzzed loudly in my ear, then touched the top of my head, lifting up my hair. I raised my hands to swat at it, but encountered—nothing. It was there one instant, then gone. It sounded and felt like one of our large Ohio locusts, size-wise at least. They grew to a couple inches long and were very loud, not to mention gross! Only something that big could make that loud a sound—and lift my hair! But nothing was there. And I realized suddenly, this had happened twice before in this same spot in the past week, although I'd shrugged it off because I'd been on the run with an errand for my houseguests. Now it was quiet here—quiet, and also very obvious: there *was* no bug. This was something new, something that had never happened before in the house, which had been haunted since we'd moved in many years ago. I'd also never previously dealt with this feeling as a paranormal investigator or psychic. If it was some sort of spirit communication, it was a new, unfamiliar method!

"James, did you touch my hair? I felt and heard a heavy vibration, like wings! Was that you?" I talked out loud to him to be sure he heard me if it was. If so, it was the third time he'd tried it that week. I'd been oblivious before this, but I finally put it together.

My husband and I discussed it for a few minutes, while I hooked up Bo Bo's leash for our walk. Just an hour earlier I'd been coming down the stairs and heard a male voice saying something. "What?" I asked my husband, who was sitting at the table below.

"I didn't say anything," he replied.

"Well I just heard *somebody* say something!" I was getting upset because this had happened a couple times already that day! After comparing notes, my husband admitted it had happened to him too.

This set the tone for my thoughts on my walk that night. I also thought about the recent investigation, trying to hear any psychic info that might come my way about it. Many times, just turning my mind to something like this led to incredible information coming to me. And of course, those thoughts then led to others—namely James's returns. I also thought about my bug phobia—and how James knew this phobia well. Sometimes, being too close to a bug would make me feel the need to spit, as though it was in my mouth. *James would know this would get my attention,* I thought, as Bo Bo and I stepped off the front porch into the night.

I live on a fairly busy street, though it was a Sunday and traffic was sparse. I love to walk at night, and my small-ish town is relatively safe and the streets well lit. With Bo Bo pulling like a maniac, I wasn't a block from my house when I saw a dark shadow on the sidewalk flying over me. I looked up just in time to see it, darker against the midnight blue sky. Puzzled, I thought maybe a plane had caused it at first, but then realized I'd heard nothing, and a plane wouldn't have made a shadow at night. *That was weird.* It put me on alert and fit right in with everything else that'd happened.

I remembered something else. That morning, while finally taking my shower in between the other six people in the house, I'd turned off the water in the shower only to hear water still running full blast. I threw back the shower curtain and saw the hot water faucet on the sink wide open and gushing. I hadn't yet used the sink at all. This had never happened before either. The handles weren't bad or loose. There just was no real explanation for it, other than James.

We'd always held the JSMS the anniversary week of James's death. This year was the third anniversary, but be-cause of the way the calendar fell, the JSMS was a little early, on Saturday the 25th. It hit me then! It had been exactly three years ago, August 26, to the minute, *this very night*, that James had been hit by the drunk driver. He died four days later, never waking from the coma.

I thought about the coincidence of the "bug," the voices, the faucets, the shadow, and wondered. Could having all James's friends here on this anniversary of the tragedy have somehow connected with him and brought him back to us again? These new occurrences had been almost as intense as the ones right after he'd died, when we'd had no doubt it was him. And my neighbor's story of him pacing the driveway fit right in.

So many mysteries in life, I thought. I loved James as much as ever; death didn't change that. I wondered if it would ever fade, as a little bit of the pain finally had.

I breathed in the cool night air, somber now, and tried to ignore the dense shadow that seemed to be standing at the end of a long dark fence on my way home, telling myself it was only my imagination. Spooked, though, my skin prickled and tingled as I went past nervously.

———

James had been on my mind a lot after all this, and the next day, after I grabbed a fast-food meal at a drive-through, I passed by our local park, and nostalgia—the good kind—struck me. I decided to eat there, and I pulled in. I parked at the top of the hill and climbed up on one of the picnic tables in a covered shelter, sitting on the tabletop with my feet on the seat. A beautiful hillside covered with mature oak trees stretched out before me, and the sounds of the merry-go-round and children's laughter drifted up from the park below, carried on a gentle breeze. *So peaceful, so beautiful*, I thought. Waves of memories and emotions hit me, and I fell into my habit of talking out loud to James.

"Ahh, James, remember all the times we came here? You wanted to live here when you were little, you loved it so much." Many days I'd left the dishes in the sink and floors unswept, just to be able to take him to the park. My rheumatoid arthritis had made me face mortality at the young age of twenty-four, and that taught me to believe it was more important to lavish James with love than do the day's dishes. I really didn't think I'd live a very long life, so every moment was precious and weighted with that belief.

I looked down to be sure of my footing and jumped off the picnic table. I walked to the nearest tree and leaned on it as I let the memories flood back. There was the football stadium below where James got in his first fight; a kid from another town started it because James walked on the opposing team's side of the stadium, unaware of the unspoken rules. Just past the stadium were the kiddie rides I took him on as a little baby. In the opposite direction was the pool where I'd drop James off with a friend each summer as he got older. Again, the unfairness of his death struck me. I guarded against allowing these feelings in every single day, but sometimes, especially when alone like this, they all came rushing back, as though making up for lost time. I still missed him so much.

With a sigh, I walked back to the picnic table and stepped up on the seat again, but I saw something dark beside my right foot. I turned and plopped down on the tabletop again, reaching for the small object. It was a black guitar pick! Where in the world did that come from! I picked it up, astonished, and saw that it had a fancy scrolled "W" on it, in white. I was flabbergasted. The black pick stood out against the scuffed wood of the picnic table seat—it had *not* been there just a couple minutes before. I would have seen it! I'd bought James a Washburn guitar when he'd first started playing, and he used it until his death. I wondered if this "W" stood for Washburn. This was exactly the kind of pick James used.

Once again, I felt James was making his presence known, maybe responding to my talking to him. His life had consisted of music and rollerblading, and this guitar pick was the perfect way to get my attention. Apports are objects that can be moved from place to place by a spirit, or even materialize out of thin air. James had done this right after he died, when a white feather came floating from my living room ceiling—when there were no feathers anywhere around that could've explained this. *Maybe James was trying hard to make himself known.* By placing this guitar pick on the bench where I'd been sitting. It worked.

"I know I need to try to let you go, James," I whispered, "but I'll never *really* be able to let you go—you're still a part of me, the best part of my life—you'll always be with me." I smiled as I looked at the pick. "Thanks for the pick," I told him. I treasure the gift.

Maybe the average skeptic wouldn't have taken this as a direct message from James, but I'd already been given too much direct evidence to doubt it. Letting go of James was still hard. And I wasn't too sure he wanted me to let go.

10

MOURNING DEATH (YOUR OWN)

Sometimes history tells us only about the events that result in tragedy, but not the aftermath. This is a story about what happened after a tragedy that formed the backdrop for a generation. About the haunting that resulted.

In 1970, the unrest on college campuses drove the evening news stories: protest marches, burnings of ROTC buildings, and all the trappings of the anti-war movement were beamed nightly into living rooms across the country in living color. Here in my home state of Ohio, the culmination of a series of events at Kent State University forever destroyed what was left of the innocence of the baby-boom generation.

On May 4, 1970, the National Guard fired into a group of student protesters, killing four of them and wounding nine more. Two of the dead had participated in the protests, but the other two were simply walking to their next class. One of the dead was an honor student at Kent State who had participated in the protest. She was also only nineteen years old.

It was a warm and sunny spring day as I drove to see Mem (short for her given name of Memory), to hear a story she wanted to tell me. Mem greeted me at the door with a big smile and we caught up on each other's news as I set up my voice recorder. I'd known Mem for quite some time, as she was my cousin Joyce's sister-in-law. But I'd never heard her ghost stories.

Mem brought iced tea right away, and it was refreshing on such a hot day. We made small talk while we sipped our beverages in her cozy and spotless living room. Finally, I told her I was ready to record her story, and she joked it might make her nervous, once the pressure was on. I reassured her that everyone else felt the same way, but it had always turned out good—so far at least. I turned on the recorder, and she began.

Mem was a student at Kent State in 1970, and the girl who was shot and killed by the National Guard lived about three doors down from her at their dormitory. The dorm was named Engleman Hall, and it was an M-shaped building that had mostly single rooms and just a few doubles. Both the girl and Mem each had a single room.

The back of Engleman Hall looked out on the commons where the riots started. Then above that was a hill;

Blanket Hill is what the students called it, because in warm weather they would all spread blankets out on the hill and sit in the sun.

I told Mem I'd never seen Kent's main campus, but had heard a lot of stories from those who went to college there.

Memory told me that this particular story had never been told before, at least *she'd* never heard it, or read it anywhere. Only those who lived there at the time would even know about it, unless, of course, it still goes on today. Mem didn't even know if that building was still used as a dorm.

Mem wasn't a close friend of the girl, but they knew each other well enough to say hi when they passed in the hallway. Of course, it was a terrible shock to them all when she was shot and killed. They were all so young.

The girl was only nineteen, and they all thought it was terrible to die at that age, so full of life and promise. For many of the students, it was their first experience with death.

Kent held a mothers' weekend each year in the spring, for students to invite their mothers up. Memory's mom and her friend's mom came up that year, the first year after the shootings. Memory's mother was there in the room with her, along with Mem's friend, and her mother too. The festivities Kent had held that day were over, and it was about 9:00 in the evening. The small group was sitting around the room talking, when all of a sudden, Mem's mother said, "Listen—someone's crying!"

I got a little cold chill as Mem said this.

They all quieted down in the dorm room, and the others could hear it too, just the clear, distinct sound of sobbing coming from somewhere. But Mem and her friend knew this sound very well, as they'd both heard it before. *All* of the students who lived there had heard it, and they'd all talked about it—and many times, they'd gone in search of it, trying to pinpoint where the crying was coming from.

The first time Mem and her friends heard it, some of them went out with the thought that somebody was very upset and maybe they could help in some way. Maybe just try to find whoever it was and do something about it. But it wasn't coming from a room. It was coming from everywhere; it was in the hall and seemed to be all around them. The dormmates walked up and down the halls trying to find who was crying—and then the crying would stop. Then sometimes it would start up again just as they went back into their rooms.

So Mem's mother and her friend's mom were both sitting there with them on that mothers' weekend, witnessing the crying that all the students had grown accustomed to.

"Don't you hear that person crying?" Mem's mother asked her. "Shouldn't you go see if you can help, or do something?"

Mem and her friend just looked at each other.

"Mom, we think it's *her* crying, the girl who was shot," Mem told her mom. "We've all heard it before and have walked up and down trying to pinpoint where it's coming from, but we never can. We've all sort of decided it's her, crying over her death."

Her mother was shocked at hearing this. "I don't believe it," she said. "That's someone here on this floor! C'mon, let's go out and see who it is."

Mem and her friend just looked at each other again and shrugged. So both their mothers led the way, and the girls followed, searching up and down the hall as the crying came from everywhere and nowhere on that weekend very near the first anniversary of the girl's tragic death. Finally, Mem's mom gave up and they all went back to her room. Her mother admitted that she believed Mem was right, that it really *was* the girl who'd died. Her mom was actually very open to these kinds of things, once all other avenues were explored.

I felt such sadness at this story.

The college girls had all been hearing the girl crying off and on for that first year after her death. But Mem doesn't remember it happening after that first year. For the rest of her life, Mem's mother mentioned the crying to her every so often. It had made an impression on her. All Mem knows is that it made quite an impression on *her*, as she'd never experienced anything like that before, at least not to that degree.

Mem and I sat lost in thought at this tragic young girl, mourning her previous carefree college life.

I hope that this poor sad girl went to the light and gave up her attachment to the site of her appalling death, even though she did mourn the loss of her life for at least that first year. This is one of the most heartbreaking stories of a haunting I've ever heard.

————

Our tea was half gone, and though I was still stuck in the gloom of the previous story, I shook it off, remembering what I came for. I asked Mem if she had any more for me.

Lucky for me, Mem did.

The house Mem grew up in was part of her grandparents' home. After her grandparents died, her parents inherited the house and built an addition, a split-level. So the basement section was original to the house when it was Mem's grandma and grandpa's. As a kid, she used to play down there, fondly recalling the cubbyholes, tools, workbench, and other fun stuff. There was even a fake wall that when you pressed on the right spot, it would open into a room with shelves.

One day, Mem was alone in the house, down in the basement doing something. She heard footsteps come in upstairs and start walking around, in both the bedroom and kitchen area. Mem's brother was ten years younger than her and still in elementary school, so she figured it was him upstairs and that she'd better go check on him. She went up and looked around everywhere, even outside, but her brother wasn't there. She wasn't really scared; she just sort of figured it was her grandpa.

Mem's brother grew up to be a total skeptic, but even *he'd* heard the walking one day. This was when he was older—Mem had moved away by then. Her brother was in his bedroom, just five or six steps up in the split-level part of the house. He heard someone walking up from the same area Mem had heard it before. Mem's brother thought it was the dog, then realized the dog was on the bed with him! Mem said her brother never even mentioned this to her until years later.

There was also a light over the kitchen table—it was the original light in the house, back when Mem's grandma and grandpa lived there. Her grandpa had been really proud of the house; he'd picked it out, and it was his baby. He was very proud of certain things like that, and he took good care of everything.

Long after her grandpa had died, the light was getting old, and definitely had seen better days. It was one of those lights that you could pull down closer to the table, or push back up. It finally got to where you would move the light up, and it would slowly slide back down. It just wouldn't stay up any longer.

One night, Mem's mom got exasperated at her husband and said, "If my dad were here, that light would be fixed!" And somehow, by the next day, it was! But Mem's dad swore *he* never fixed it. And really, there wasn't any time he *could've* fixed it between Mem's mother putting the challenge out there and the time her dad was away at work, and then when the light was fixed. So the rest of the family always believed Grandpa came back and fixed the light!

"I bet he did!" I laughed. "That was a challenge if I ever heard one!"

Mem then told me a story about Dover Dam, near where I live. It was a huge Army Corps of Engineers project from the 1920s and was built across a large river that runs between our towns.

Each summer when Mem was home from college, a bunch of her friends would get together at night and go somewhere, to the lake or wherever they could think of to go. One night they drove out to Dover Dam. They parked their cars down on the lower ground level, via a small access road that led to a picnic area beside the river. While out sitting at the table, they suddenly got a weird feeling. A couple of them looked up and saw a shadow of a man standing at the railing near a workroom in the dam. But this was late at night, and the workroom was closed. The shadow was visible under the lights, but you couldn't see any features or details of his face, just a thick, black shadow outlined in the lights. They turned to tell their friends, looked back, and he was gone. There were no cars anywhere around, and the dam is in the middle of nowhere, so it's not like someone would be walking by. It was really creepy and they all got spooked by it and left. Later, when they found out about the workmen who had been killed while building the dam, they were pretty freaked out.

I explained that they may have witnessed a shadow person, considered a type of paranormal entity that some believe is malevolent. Others believe that some spirits present themselves this way. There are differing opinions in the paranormal investigations field, and the truth is, no one really knows for sure.

"It was pretty creepy that night, a real cringe-worthy feeling!" Mem added.

There are so many unexplained things; that's the only thing we *can* know for sure sometimes. Talking about these kinds of experiences often brings up other old memories for people, and Mem was no exception. She thought of something she hadn't remembered in years. Mem had a professor at seminary who was very close to her; she babysat his kids and was treated as part of their family. Mem graduated in June, and in September she was in bed sleeping one night when there was a huge thump against the wall and a loud crashing sound along with a vibration that woke her up. It was way too loud a sound for a bird. Mem was on the second floor, so she couldn't figure out what it was that had caused this. After searching around and finding nothing out of place, she finally went back to sleep. The next morning, Mem got a call from another professor telling her that her professor friend had died at the same time the noise hit the house and woke her. It seemed far more than just a coincidence.

I explained to Mem that this actually seems to happen a lot. Sometimes those who pass away seem to want to let us know they've died, especially when their deaths were unexpected or sudden. I've also found a lot of stories where a sick relative has hung on and on—until their loved ones gave them permission to go. And sometimes it seems they won't go if you're there with them; they don't want to leave with you there. This happened with my own grandma. She was only a couple months away from turning one hundred. She always told everyone she wanted to make it to that centennial birthday. My dad had been visiting her in the hospital, and she was doing fine. She'd been admitted because of some minor problems. My dad talked to his mother for quite a while, and then he told her he'd be back later. He'd no sooner left Grandma's room and started down the hallway, when a nurse came out of her room and called to Dad. He turned back, and she told him Gram had died, just after the nurse walked in.

"That happened with my grandma too!" Mem told me. Her grandmother lived in an apartment just a few blocks away from them when she was young. Her grandmother was ill and nearing the end. Hospice had been contacted and they brought in a hospital bed. Mem's mother visited her grandma and told her it was okay to go. She told her, "I'll be okay. My husband and family will watch over me." Mem's mother had ridden her bike to her grandma's house, as it was just a few blocks. After her mother gave Mem's grandma permission to leave, she told her she had to go home and get dinner ready for her husband and family, and she left. She just got home and got the call from hospice that her mother had just passed away.

I finished my tea, thanking Mem for making time to tell me her experiences. As I drove away, I thought about my next interview appointment. So many ghost stories, so little time—and I had an appointment to hear another one the next day.

11

COLONIAL GHOSTS

My friend Bart has a long history with Schoenbrunn, the colonial settlement where the terrible massacre of innocents took place two centuries ago. I'd met Bart years ago at a restaurant where I was performing. I'd also seen him perform many times in various plays he'd starred in. A talented actor and singer, Bart was well known in my area, and we also had mutual friends. My cousin Joyce had worked with him when she was very young. Joyce had met Bart when she was an usher for an outdoor drama that showcases the story of the massacre. Bart has performed various parts in the drama over the years.

The drama is held just across the valley from the reconstructed colonial village of Schoenbrunn. The play takes place during the summer months at an outdoor amphitheater surrounded by forest and hills. One day while Joyce and I talked about her latest ghost doll, she told me that Bart had some stories to tell me.

I drove to meet Bart where he was doing some tech work in preparation for a play. When I walked into the theater, I met him coming up the aisle. We hugged and Bart caught me up on what he'd been up to.

"I've been pretty busy lately. I'm now playing the lead in a couple plays and also doing some directing." I told him I couldn't wait to see him in the lead role he'd been playing at the outdoor drama. Bart thanked me and told me he was enjoying the work, then got down to business.

I explained that I wanted to hear anything about his brushes with the other side, and Bart began to give me a little background about theater first. He explained that a lot of preparation goes into putting on a theatrical performance, particularly an outdoor drama. Early on, auditions for various cast members take place, then later on the actors who win parts arrive from all over the country and live here for the summer months of the production. Many of the new cast members each year are from other states, so they know next to nothing about the history of our area of Ohio. They know nothing about the massacre, the subject of the outdoor drama. So a tradition has sprung up among Bart and the local actors. They take the entire cast down to the mass grave of the villagers (all Christian Indians) of Schoenbrunn. Bart always does this on opening night after the first performance.

The actors take flowers to the graves of the massacred villagers, and they promise to tell their story so they'll never be forgotten. The actors want to get their blessing while telling their story during the play. They sing the final song of the production, a Moravian hymn, and then they walk solemnly through the grounds. They also take a list of the victims' names and read them out loud, just to let them know the living still think of them.

Bart said they finish by talking about the history and answering any questions about the massacre from the out-of-state cast members.

I told Bart that it was a really nice gesture, and it went a long way toward making up for the lack of respect the massacre victims originally experienced, paranormally speaking. That sort of acknowledgment is believed to calm negative energy at a site of a terrible tragedy. Bart instinctively knew this already, and he agreed with me.

The caretakers of the grounds and the museum are great supporters of the production and know all of the local cast members very well. Bart said they usually take the cast members down there at least once before the production starts to introduce them and teach them a little of the history. The caretakers always give the new cast members a tour.

On this particular opening night, once the show was over, Bart and his fellow actors all went down to do their yearly ceremony. The show ends late, so it was close to midnight when they arrived. The buildings that have been reconstructed—the church and the cooper's cabin where the massacre took place—are kept padlocked at night. The cast members placed their flowers, read the names of the massacre victims, and then sang their hymn. When they finished, they walked over toward the buildings. One of the cast members came running back to tell Bart that the padlock on the church had been left open. So Bart walked over to check the cooper's cabin, and sure enough, it was unlocked too. Bart knew they were always kept locked at night. The buildings had a simple hinge-type hasp, and it was open, but the padlock was on the hinge, closed and locked.

It was also pretty dark that night—there were no lights. Suddenly, Bart and his fellow actors all began to feel a heavy presence; they could absolutely sense the victims with them, there in the dark. It was electric. Bart had never felt this before, not in all the previous trips he'd made down there on opening nights. Everyone there felt it and were in awe. The new members had never been in the buildings at night, and it was an entirely different feeling than in daylight.

After staying a while, they began to head back to their cars, and Bart silently thanked Brenda, the caretaker, for leaving the doors open for them. It was a nice gesture, but not altogether unexpected, as Brenda is one of their greatest supporters and knew they came down on opening night.

As one of the last to leave the site, Bart closed the doors to the unlocked buildings as best he could; he couldn't lock them since the padlocks were already locked.

The next night, Brenda and her husband came to the outdoor performance. Afterward, Bart approached her to thank her for her thoughtfulness.

"Brenda, I want to thank you," Bart began.

She got a puzzled look on her face. "For what?"

"For leaving the buildings open last night for our ceremony." Her face dropped.

"What?" she answered, looking puzzled. And then she told Bart she hadn't!

"But the padlocks were on the loops—locked—and the doors were open!" Bart told her.

"We locked them, Bart, just the same as we always do."

Confused, Bart knew this was impossible because the padlocks were locked on the hinges!

When he explained this, Brenda smiled again and told Bart they hadn't left them unlocked. Then she added that the locks had been locked correctly when they'd arrived there that morning! Brenda said she wouldn't even have known about this at all, except for Bart telling her. Bart was shocked. Then suddenly he knew—he knew for sure, that *they* were with them that opening night—the massacred villagers. Bart knew they weren't just imagining their presence that night. The massacred villagers were there for the actors that night, and Bart knows now that they really do appreciate their respect.

Bart smiled, still touched by the spirits' gesture that opening night.

"I believe they unlocked the buildings for us." Bart thought for a moment and then began to tell me another story of the massacre site.

A lady who came down to the site one day was a descendant of one of the massacre victims. She'd traveled a long way to finally see the spot where her relative met his end all those years ago. But she told the caretakers she'd been having a dream, over and over, about a flower. This was late winter, and our area had just had a large snowstorm. Because this woman had traveled so far, the caretakers walked through the snow with her, pointing out various points of interest, until they all finally arrived at the massacre site. Beside an old tree, sticking up through the snow was the flower the visitor had seen repeatedly in her dreams, and just as in the woman's dream, the flower was in full, beautiful bloom! This was a seemingly impossible event in the dead of winter. The descendant believed that this is where her ancestor had fallen, and somehow this was her ancestor's message to her.

Bart believes the spirits of the victims still make themselves known, and he also thinks they still walk the area around Schoenbrunn. Bart told me that up in the woods behind the outdoor drama site, the horses spook a lot for no reason at all. Many times, while on a horse up there, Bart could feel the horse getting fidgety and edgy, and when he'd look around—it's all wide open up there—there was never anything there. Bart said there was one horse that wouldn't go into that area at all. One night, while Bart was playing a Native American, he was on the horse backstage (backstage is actually a hill leading into the forest with a flat clearing at the top) and Bart wasn't really paying attention. The horse threw him off. He had to go after the horse pretty quickly, as his next cue was coming, and he needed to ride the horse back down the hill and onto the stage. But that horse simply would not enter the clearing. He had thrown Bart as they'd approached the clearing together, then afterward, the horse ran to just the other side of the clearing and stopped—waiting for him! Bart could not get him to cross back over the clearing. And when playing Native Americans, the actors ride bareback, so there's nothing to grab onto. Bart laughed at recounting his dilemma that night.

Bart explained that many people hear things up there too. Some have heard screaming, and one person saw a figure running through the woods. Once they remember that this is the area where all the massacre victims once walked, it begins to get to everybody a little bit. The location is just across from the village of Schoenbrunn, not even a mile away.

I mentioned that Bart seemed to be very intuitive himself, very open, from what I was sensing. This may also be part of the reason Bart has had so many experiences.

"Yes, I think I am," he agreed. "From the time I was a young child, I've had various things happen around me."

Bart was always afraid of his bedroom, so he slept in the living room. His mom used to get mad at him because of it, but that's where he wanted to sleep—period. He just would not go into his room.

Bart remembered one night when he was in the sixth grade, something woke him up while he was sleeping in the living room. He got up to get a drink in the kitchen, and when he turned around and looked toward his room, he saw a little girl walk into his bedroom. Bart dropped the glass and it shattered. He never saw her again.

Bart told me he now owned his childhood house and that his mom had passed away there too. She passed away in that same bedroom—Bart's old room, the one that he used to be so afraid of. Bart had just told his mother it was okay to go, that he'd be okay, and then she fell asleep and peacefully passed away about forty-five minutes later. I told Bart I'd just interviewed others who told similar stories about their parents.

Bart believed his mom came back a few times too. All Bart's friends loved his mom, and they often played cards together. In the kitchen was a radio cassette player—Bart, his friends, and his mom would all sit in the kitchen playing cards and listening to it. Bart's mom always turned the radio on because she liked to hear it while they played. After his mom passed away, Bart's friends were in town, and they got together at Bart's house. They started playing cards that night. Suddenly, the radio turned on by itself. Bart's friends nervously glanced at him, so he got up and turned it off. Bart sat back down again, picked up his hand, and the radio came back on! Bart's friends just stared at him, shocked. "It's Mom," he told them, and he just knew that it was. And they knew she was letting them know she was there. After that, Bart's mom would also open the doors a lot, and Bart thought it was so he would know she was around.

Bart's mom had had a necklace he'd given her that had been lost for years. His mother couldn't find it anywhere and it upset her greatly. After she died, Bart decided to give some of her things to those he thought would like to have them. He went to her jewelry box, opened it up, and lying right on top like it was placed there for him to find was that necklace! It had been missing for years and she'd hunted everywhere for it. Bart thinks that after his mom died, she found out where it was and put it there in the jewelry box for him to find.

Bart is a true believer in our loved ones coming back to reassure us that they are still aware, and still here for us. I thanked Bart for all the great information, and we said our goodbyes. As I made my way out, I remembered another story a friend recently told me about the Schoenbrunn area. This friend lives just a little way from Schoenbrunn Village, just on the other side of the river.

I ran into him one day at the store, and we somehow got to talking about my favorite subject. He told me that several times he'd woken up to a white-haired man with a long beard at the foot of his bed, staring at him with a scowl on his face. The strangest thing about this man is that he was dressed in the clothing and knee breeches of the late eighteenth century, just as the missionaries and the Christian Indians would've dressed. My friend also keeps finding his back door open—even though he keeps it locked. He will feel it getting cold in his living room and then go check, and sure enough, the back door is open again.

I believe this ghost in knee breeches may very well be one of the early inhabitants of Schoenbrunn. This spirit probably wonders who this stranger is, camping here by *their* river, and encroaching upon *their* land. To them, it's still 1782 in Schoenbrunn.

12

TILL DEATH DO US PART?

I set up an interview to meet Al, the golf partner of a man who had worked part time for me. Al and his wife, Chris, were a middle-aged couple married for more than forty years. They'd had one of those lifelong love affairs you sometimes hear about. Their love had lasted throughout their entire marriage—and went on to survive Chris's death.

Chris had been a big believer in the afterlife and in ghosts and spirits. The couple had attended a psychic fair once and had been told that they were brother and sister in another incarnation, which caused a lot of hilarity on their more amorous nights.

When Chris's mother passed away years earlier, Chris believed she'd been sent a sign. That first year after her mom died, Al and Chris stayed up late one night watching a movie and then each fell asleep in their recliners. They awoke to a strange sound coming from somewhere in the house, but they couldn't determine its location. Finally, they traced the sound to the kitchen, and Chris recognized it. She owned a plate that played "Happy Birthday," which the family used for their cakes at birthday celebrations.

Chris's birthday was the following day, and as she dug deep in the cupboard for the plate, knowing it was impossible to turn the plate on without physically doing so, she wondered if her mom might've been involved. At the same time, she said aloud, "I might've thought Mom was telling me happy birthday if she'd only waited one more day!" Al looked at his watch and said, "Chris! It's after midnight! It's your birthday!" Chris just smiled as she realized Al was right! Then she thanked her mom, knowing her mother had somehow turned the plate on to send her birthday wishes. The plate never again played by itself.

Al had his own experiences with the paranormal return of loved ones. Al's father had clinically died years earlier and was revived, literally brought back to life. After that, he was never afraid to die, stating that it was a wonderful white light. Al's dad lived many more years after that. Finally, time passed, disease and illness took their toll, and Al's father neared death again. He had been in a coma for six months before he passed away, and Al's mother went to visit him every day. One cold winter's night, Al was home, asleep in bed. Suddenly something woke him up, and as he lay there wondering what it was, a huge blast of ice-cold air blew through the house, almost as though a window had been opened in the wintry weather. *That's Dad!* Al thought. A moment later, the telephone rang and it was Al's mother calling to tell him that his father had just passed away. "I already know, Mom," Al told her.

More recently, Al's mother died, and Al believes she too came back to let her children know she was okay. The week before his mother went into her final coma, she told Al's sisters she'd dreamt of a beautiful banquet with flowers, food, and a table set with the finest silver and china. She said she'd never seen anything so gorgeous and perfect. The hospice nurse told Al's mom that maybe it meant they were preparing it for her, that maybe soon it was *her* time to go be with her husband. But Al's mother said no.

"It's only for men this time," she told her daughters and the puzzled nurse. "No women are going."

Al's sister grabbed the paper the next day to look at the obituaries, and sure enough, only men had died that day in their large city!

Al's sisters had been their mother's primary caregivers along with hospice, and they were all staying at their mother's house. When the brothers and sisters were kids, they had a rule at home that whenever any of them went anywhere, they were to call home, let it ring once, and hang up, so as not to lose their dime in the pay phone. That was their code that they had arrived safely at their destinations.

Al's sister walked into their mother's room just as his other sister told her she thought their mom had just passed away. As they stood there trying to discern if their mother was still breathing, the phone rang once! They knew then that their mom had arrived safely and was letting them know.

————

Al and his wife, Chris, had been high school sweethearts, and once their children were grown, they began enjoying their midlife years together. Both Al's and Chris's favorite activity was a vacation cruise to the Caribbean, where they could snorkel, enjoy the ocean, and savor the fabulous food. Chris felt it was the best holiday any woman could have, and Al went along with her wishes.

The year of Chris's death was no different. She and Al had been looking forward to escaping the cold weather for the balmy tropics. The trip began uneventfully enough until the third day, when the ship was anchored on the open sea, and Al and Chris went snorkeling. It was a beautiful morning as usual in the region. A large catamaran filled with a group of like-minded cruise-ship guests steered Al and Chris a distance away from the ship. The catamaran was large enough to hold quite a few passengers and even had a bar for the guests' enjoyment.

The blue water was warm, the sun was shining, and the fish were plentiful. There was a lot to see. Al and Chris enjoyed their favorite hobby together on a near-perfect day.

Al had an underwater camera that he liked to tinker with each time they went diving. It was a good one that took great pictures both in and out of the water.

After snorkeling a little while, Chris said she was tired, and Al asked if she was ready to quit.

"Yes, I think I'm going back to the catamaran to relax and have a drink," Chris told her husband.

"All right. I think I'm gonna stay out just a little while longer, and I'll see you back there soon." This was unusual because Al had always called it quits once Chris was done snorkeling.

Al watched Chris swim away, heading for the catamaran. On impulse, he began to snap a few pictures of his wife with her mask and vest on as she swam back. It was about 10:00 in the morning.

Al continued to snorkel for a just little while longer and then swam back to the catamaran. As he tried to come onboard, he was told there had been a medical emergency and he would have to wait. So Al went back out to snorkel a bit more. Soon, someone from the crew called out Al's name, and he swam back and was allowed onboard. There was a major commotion on deck, but all he could see was a group of people gathered around something. Suddenly, he saw that they were gathered around Chris, giving her CPR! The crew told Al that Chris had no sooner climbed back onboard than she'd been felled by a major heart attack. The crew and others worked on Chris for a long time, but were unable to revive her. Apparently she had died instantly.

Of course for Al, this was a nightmare scenario of epic proportions. He spent the rest of the cruise sitting with his wife's body each night in the ship's morgue. Although the captain said they would bring a helicopter to pick Al up, Chris's body would have to be shipped, and Al just didn't want to be separated from her. It made for some uncomfortable moments with the other guests onboard, but Al didn't care. He decided to wait, along with his wife's body, until the cruise was over and he could accompany Chris home. His friends thought it was pretty morbid, but Al thought Chris would've wanted him to stay. Little did Al know that the pictures he'd snapped of his wife that day were her last moments of existence on earth.

Al's grief was as deep as anyone would expect after the sudden death of a soul mate. And it was bittersweet for it to happen in such an idyllic setting where the couple had shared so much and had so many good times. Al told himself that Chris had died doing what she loved with the person she loved most in the place she loved best. And Al tried to move on as best he could—alone. Six months had passed by the time Al finally got around to giving the film from that fateful day to his son to get developed. One night a while afterward, Al's son came to him and asked if his father had seen the pictures he'd dropped off at the house. Al hadn't. He didn't want to be reminded, so he put them away without looking. His son got them from the drawer.

"Look at this one. What do you see?" Al's son asked. It was the picture of Chris swimming back to the catamaran, the one Al had taken mere moments before her death. A white opaque shape was rising up out of her body and heading into the blue sky above—with what appeared, almost, to be wings sprouting from it! Al felt that somehow this was Chris's spirit leaving her body. I explained to Al what many in the paranormal world believe. In some deaths where there is pain involved, such as a heart attack or an accident where someone burns to death, many believe that the soul is taken from the body beforehand, so no pain is felt. The body continues to move and act as it normally would, but the *spirit* is gone. I told Al he may have caught Chris's spirit moving on to the light that day she died.

Somehow, Al got through Chris's death, her funeral, and the aftermath, and he grieved along with family and friends. That fateful cruise and Chris's subsequent death had been in early November, and Al dreaded the upcoming holidays. But Chris had loved the holiday season, especially Christmas Eve—the night their whole family got together and celebrated, with hors d'oeuvres and a big meal. Chris had always planned the details of their get-together.

Al decided the best way to honor Chris's memory was to continue the tradition—with one exception. They had always teased Chris mercilessly about the fact that each year, no matter how early she planned to serve the hors d'oeuvres on Christmas Eve, they always ended up being ready at the same time as dinner. This first year without Chris, only six weeks after her death, as the entire family stood around talking after they'd arrived, Al brought up Chris's traditionally late hors d'oeuvres. This little foible of Chris's had been the source of much merriment in their family over the years.

"Chris, this year, I'm in charge, so we are having hors d'oeuvres at 6:00!" Al joked. As soon as Al announced his early hors d'oeuvres time schedule, the lights flashed! Al's son, daughter-in-law, and everyone else there grew very quiet. And then the lights went completely out. Finally, they came back on.

"I can't believe that just happened," said Al's daughter-in-law.

Al decided to answer Chris right then and there. "Chris, I don't care, this year I'm in charge, and we're having hors d'oeuvres at 6:00!" They all laughed, and Al and his family truly felt Chris's presence there with them at that first Christmas Eve without her.

That first year without Chris was tough on Al. There are always the "firsts" to get through: the first holidays, the first birthdays, and so on. Al had played in a golf league for many years each Thursday evening during summer, and Al and Chris started the tradition that golf night was also pizza night. Somehow, although her timing of the hors d'oeuvres was always off, Chris's timing on pizza/golf night was impeccable. Nearly every time Al walked into their home at 8:00 p.m. after golfing on Thursday, the oven timer would go off just as he came through the door. And then Al would take out the pizza Chris had made for their supper.

When the first Thursday of golf league started up that spring, Al was sad as he made his way home, remembering pizza night. It brought it all back and made Al think about how badly he missed Chris. When Al opened the door to his house, the oven timer was going off! This was a definitive moment for Al. He knew for sure Chris was telling him she was there, and she missed their pizza night too. Al shut the timer off and spoke aloud to his deceased wife, thanking her and telling her how he missed their lives together. It was an electronic timer that had to be set by hand, and Al lived there alone, so there was no way it could go off by itself.

The oven timer has never gone off since that night when Chris set it for Al. But on that first Thursday evening of the golf league, Chris seemed to know that Al needed a little sign she was okay and that she still watched over him. And that she hadn't forgotten their pizza night!

Apparently Chris was worried about the man she'd left behind. After all, he'd been the love of her life since their teenage years. Al believes Chris feels the need to check in on him and let him know she's watching over him. And that's just what Chris still does.

————

My artistic cousin Joyce has many like-minded friends. I met Joyce's friend Rae at an out-of-state event where Joyce exhibited her dolls. Rae is a young artist who also leans toward Halloween art. Of course, she asked about the book I was working on because she's almost as interested in the paranormal as I am.

"Actually, I'm interviewing friends about their ghost stories right now, Rae. You don't happen to have one, do you?" It turns out she did.

Rae's grandparents had been married for sixty-nine years. Her grandpa was in the hospital, sick with cancer, and Rae's grandma was so upset about his illness and impending death that the stress had recently landed her in the hospital too, just down the hall from her husband.

Rae's grandpa had gone into a final coma, and her mom and her mother's sister, Rae's aunt, were sitting beside his bed. Rae's mom decided to tell her father it was okay to leave—that they would look after his wife.

"Dad, you can go now, it's okay. We'll take care of Mom for you," Rae's mother said. As soon as the words left her lips, their comatose father raised his head from the pillow, gave a deep sigh, and left this earthly life. The wrinkles in his face all smoothed out, and he was the picture of peace.

The nurse came in just as this happened, checked the women's father, and then asked the two sisters if they would please wait to inform their mother that her husband had passed away.

"The doctor would like to be here with her when she's given the news," the nurse said.

Rae's mom and aunt agreed, and they decided to walk down to their mother's room to check on her while waiting for the doctor. They were shocked to see their mom with one arm raised high in the air, as if someone was holding it. Their mother had been pretty ill, and wasn't extremely alert at that moment. But she had a story to tell them.

"Daddy was just here—he rubbed my back," said the old woman. This was something their dad had always done for their mom. "But he's gone now—he had to go. He just left," their mother told her daughters. Rae's young face showed her emotion.

"My mom and her sister just looked at each other. They knew their dad had come to say goodbye to their mom, and rubbed her back while he was at it too."

I told Rae it was a great story, and we sat in silence for a minute. It is strange how in some families, returns seem to be the norm, yet not at all in others.

13

THE CHILDREN OF DEATH

The spirits of children seem to be common visitors to our realm. Sometimes they're children who've died of illness or accident who don't seem to know they're dead. They are known to visit their old homes long after their families have died and gone to their reward. But I've also recently heard of a more unusual phenomenon taking place in several local nursing homes, and I believe it may happen on a much wider scale all around the world.

Roughly 4 percent of Americans over sixty-five years old are in nursing homes. The percentage increases with age, so it goes without saying, there are a lot of nursing homes in the United States.

The first time I heard about the children of death, it was from Megan, a friend's daughter who works in a large nursing home in my town. This incident took place not long after Megan was hired. One day one of the elderly residents, Mr. Miller, didn't want to go down to the dining room to eat. Mr. Miller had a weather radio beside his bed on a small nightstand. It was his pride and joy, one of the few things he had left, and no one was allowed to touch it. He kept it pushed far back against the wall at the rear of the table.

"Mr. Miller, why don't you want to come down to lunch?" asked the nurse who had come in with my friend's daughter, Megan, the aide.

"Because these dang kids keep messing with my radio! They're gonna break it! They're jumping on the bed and giving me all kinds of grief!"

The nurse soothingly told the old man that there was no one in the room but him.

"What!? Can't you see them? They're gonna tear everything up!" the old man said, pointing to the far corner.

The nurse told him she couldn't see them and asked where exactly they were. Mr. Miller pointed to the chair in the far corner where the nurse had just seated herself. "One's under your chair."

The nurse jumped up uneasily and peered underneath the chair. She told her patient sternly that there was nothing there.

"Now they're jumping on the bed! Can't you see them?" Mr. Miller reached toward his precious radio. "Look. They've got it almost pushed off the edge." Megan noticed the weather radio was all the way to the front of the man's table and was about to fall over the ledge. Puzzled, she moved it back into place, reassuring the old gentleman that it should be safe now.

Finally after much cajoling, they got Mr. Miller into a wheelchair, and another aide wheeled him down to lunch. The nurse and Megan left, and a new aide began changing Mr. Miller's bed and cleaning the room. This aide was aware of the story Mr. Miller had been telling about the children in his room. Since the old man had been refusing to leave his room for a while, most of the staff knew about it as well.

Suddenly the aide came out of Mr. Miller's room and called to the other girls in the area. "You've got to see this." They all came into Mr. Miller's room, and the aide walked to the other side of the bed and pulled the curtain back. The girls moved in closer to see what she was pointing at. There on the glass was a perfectly shaped child's handprint! Mr. Miller did not *have* any young family members, nor did anyone else who had visited him. It was then that Megan learned about the death children.

The day nurse explained that the children usually come when someone's about to pass away, and they actually kept a log book at the nursing home that contained detailed written accounts about everything that happened. There had been some very strange entries about these children.

Megan was a little upset, not to mention amazed, that the death children were considered real by the staff, but she wanted to know more. She still didn't believe it.

The nurse told her that most staff members were used to them. Some nights, they did nothing but answer buzzers from patients who were being bothered by these children. Then the staff noticed that the patient deaths usually came in threes after the children showed up. Once the children came, the patient was usually within a day or two of dying. Megan could scarcely believe it and asked if the patients couldn't just be hallucinating these children for some reason, possibly dementia related.

The nurse glanced at the other aide standing there, then back at my friend's daughter, as if she was afraid to tell her. Finally, she answered that she'd seen the boy child herself.

As soon as she heard this, Megan got a cold chill and wrapped her arms around herself, and the nurse told her the story.

One night, the nurse had taken the medicine cart into a patient's room. She was checking the IV and going through her routine when she noticed a little boy peering around the cart at her. She stared, hardly able to believe what she was seeing, and then as she watched, the child just disappeared.

The aide chimed in with a story of her own. A friend of hers was working the night shift, staffing the nurses' desk, when she saw the head of a little blond girl walk past. And she continued to see the girl several more times.

Another nurse had also seen the little girl, and she got a clear view of her. She had blond hair and was dressed in a long, white old-fashioned dress.

Megan found this information nearly unbelievable and had almost dismissed it, until one day while she was talking to a nurse at another area nursing home, she decided to mention the children. That nurse smiled knowingly. "You know about the death children?" Megan asked.

"Oh yes. We see them at our nursing home too."

Megan was astounded. Apparently the phenomenon went beyond their own facility.

One night Megan had a ghostly experience of her own, although it didn't involve the children. She was in the laundry room loading the washer with linens from the rooms. Suddenly someone pressed their body, full length, up against her back. She pulled away and turned around to see which elderly resident had done such a thing, but no one was there. Panicked, she ran out and hasn't been able to bear going back in since.

Megan's stories brought back the memories of my own mother during the last weeks of her life. She continually told me children were singing to her, and sometimes she would laugh at their antics and talk about the children visiting her. I assumed she was hallucinating, as she'd had dementia for a while. Now I'm not so sure. After hearing

Megan's story, I'm a little less skeptical and wonder how many of us will deal with the death children ourselves.

———

One of the most incredible true ghost stories I've heard involved another child and was relayed to me by a friend. An area couple, Mr. and Mrs. Dolan, were local business owners who bought a grand old home on one of our town's main thoroughfares. The home was a nineteenth-century beauty, built of old stone and turreted in the late Victorian fashion. After they bought the home and moved in, sometimes when the Dolan family was in the living room watching a movie, books and DVDs would fly off the shelves. It was almost as though something wanted attention. But although several family members were becoming uneasy, they hadn't yet put two and two together. Then one day Mrs. Dolan had an experience that shook her to her core. And it left no doubt she shared her home with unseen guests. My friend relayed the story Mrs. Dolan had told her.

Mrs. Dolan had an overstuffed easy chair in the corner of her bedroom, but the slipcover she kept on it was constantly messed up. Mrs. Dolan couldn't figure this out because no one ever sat in that chair, and the family dog was kept out of her bedroom.

On this one particular day, Mrs. Dolan was cleaning, and as she reached her bedroom to tidy up, she once again noticed the easy chair in the corner. The slipcover on it was messed up again! This time, there was a dip in the seat cushion, as though someone had been sitting in it. No one was home at the time—both her kids were in school. Exasperated by this ongoing problem, Mrs. Dolan walked to the chair with both hands outstretched to tuck in the sides of the slipcover at the edges of the seat cushion. As she reached the chair and leaned down to tuck it in, a tiny but high-pitched voice loudly screamed, "*NO!*"

Mrs. Dolan jerked back, terrified. Some unseen thing was sitting in her bedroom easy chair! It sounded like a child. Now in a cold sweat, she rushed away and left the house. After her family got home, she told them about it, and they then began to take note of other things that happened. Later they found out a child had died in the house, in a fire, during the 1800s. The little girl's nightgown caught fire and she was horribly burned. The child lingered for a few days, but eventually passed away. It seems the little girl is still there—and she likes to sit in Mrs. Dolan's easy chair. But she doesn't like to be touched!

———

I was performing at one of my favorite music venues, beautiful Breitenbach Wine Cellars in Amish Country. On my break, an audience member came up to me and we began talking about music. I mentioned my son's songs and my own. Then I handed him a bookmark for my upcoming book release, joking about shameless self-promotion. This led to an answering wisecrack on his part on the order of,

"You play and write music, you write books—what *else* do you do?"—which led to me telling him about the psychic thing. Then I told him I was working on a new book about ghost stories and how I've been fascinated with them since I moved into a haunted house as a teen. The man's expression turned serious, and he suddenly crouched down beside my chair, confidentially, saying he didn't tell this story to many people for fear of being labeled crazy. I told him I understood, but added that there are many more believers these days because so many of us had also had experiences. He then hesitantly shared his story.

He and his had wife had lived in an apartment before they'd bought their home. His wife had never had any problems and never saw anything at the apartment. The man had always been a skeptic and never believed ghosts and things like that were real. Then one night while he was fast asleep, something shook the him by the shoulder. He'd been lying on his back, and he opened his eyes. Directly above him was a little girl slowly floating away from him up toward the ceiling, looking down on him. This would wake anyone up in a hurry!

The man said it was unbelievable, but he was wide awake and saw it with his own eyes, so he knew it was real. Somehow, though, he didn't have a feeling of fear. After all, it was just a little girl. She watched him the entire time as she rose to the ceiling, and then she just faded away. He never saw her at their apartment again. And he was never a skeptic again either. That did it for him—he knew ghosts were real. He told me I could use his story of the little ghost girl that woke him up.

I thanked him for telling me about his experience and then went back up to the stage to finish out my last set of music. I thought about how no matter where I happened to be, I was surrounded by ghost stories. They came in the most unlikely of places, from the unlikeliest people, and from friends and strangers alike.

———

This stranger's story brought back the memory of another incident that featured children. This one involved a nanny. I'd gone on an investigation at one of Sherri Brake's Haunted Heartland Tours events in the quaint little town of Zoar, Ohio. The town was built by German separatists in the early 1800s and was one of the first communes in the United States. There were buildings where they lived and worked, and men's and women's dorms—even husbands and wives lived separately. There was a nursery where newborns were taken after their birth and raised by designated women.

The commune also had a pious leader who made nearly all the decisions for the separatists. The members built a beautiful mansion for this leader, who promptly spurned it as too elaborate, opting to live more modestly in a smaller, plainer house. The fancier building was then used for various purposes, but at one time, a room upstairs was the designated newborn room where a nanny cared for the babies.

Most of the guests who'd attended Sherri's investigation that night had left, and a few of us were still standing behind the Number One house, the name given to the grand mansion built for the leader. Sherri had been telling the story of the woman who still haunted the nursery and the recent EVPs recorded there. The playback was of a woman's voice saying, "Shhhh." The speculation was that the long-deceased nurse of the newborns was shushing people, afraid they'd wake the babies.

Just as Sherri finished the story, she pointed to the nursery's window and someone said they saw movement. Several of us decided to go up and check it out.

I turned on my digital recorder as we climbed the stairs, and on the recorder, our tennis shoes are heard squeaking on the marble floors. We stopped in the doorway, and I held my recorder just inside the door of the nursery. I asked a question.

"Is there anyone here tonight who would like to say something?" All of us waited in complete silence with our digital recorders running. We stayed a few more minutes then walked back down to rejoin the others. When I listened to the playback, in answer to my question, a tiny female voice answers, "Me." She wanted to say something. Another digital recorder picked up the same voice. But while we stood there, it had been absolutely quiet. It gave me chills. This poor nursemaid had patiently waited over a century to be heard. She waits there for eternity, tending long-dead babies in the nursery at Zoar, wanting to say something. I wish I'd have asked her what it was.

———————

My own child's returns continued. One night after my evening walk, I settled in on the sofa with my laptop, checking the galleys for my first book. I added small parts and deleted others, getting ready for the final proofing for my publisher. I'd decided to re-read the book from the beginning with a fresh eye after having had some time away from it.

We'd just recently held our third-annual charity event in our son's name. Seeing all his old friends was always great and the full day of skating, music, and competition—all of James's favorite things—was fun. I didn't like to dwell too much on the sad reason we held the event and focused more on the happy side: raising money and seeing old friends. It had been a particularly good year, and we had a much larger crowd who came to meet a famous skater we flew in to emcee. But as always, the letdown afterward was the hardest part. A lot of busywork led up to the event, and lots of hustle and bustle surrounded it—then suddenly it was over. It was so good to see James's friends and to have a house full of young people again. I missed that, so each time, it was harder to say goodbye to them. I'd come to realize that any losses, even temporary ones, are harder to take after losing a child.

After I brought up my book files on my laptop, I found one of my favorite movies on TV, *The Exorcist*, and I settled in to do the work on my book. Bo Bo was on the pillow to my left, and the remote was on the pillow to my right. William Friedkin was the famous director of *The Exorcist*. He'd also recently directed the Matthew McConaughey movie *Killer Joe*—which through the efforts of my LA music publisher used James's song "On the Prowl" in the red band trailer. So I was particularly excited to watch *The Exorcist* again now.

I should've known I'd get overinvolved in the movie, and I did most of the proofreading of my book during the commercial breaks with the TV muted. I finally came to the chapter where James's death took place. Somehow this time when I read it back, it hit me like a sledgehammer and I lost it. It was a major meltdown. I hadn't cried so hard for a long time. I think the additional melancholy of James's friends leaving must've fueled this.

With the TV still on mute, I cried and sobbed, wallowing in my misery and asking why. At one point, I begged James to come back, to give me a sign, some definitive answer—would I really see him again in the afterlife? Was it really as we'd always been taught, God and the whole nine yards? I must've needed the emotional release of a good cry, because I'd held it in a little too long this time. Finally, the waterworks subsided, and I got up to get a tissue. I leaned against the back of the couch, wiping my eyes, still talking to James.

"I'm sorry, James, but I still miss you so bad. I'm sorry. Be at peace, honey; don't mind me." I felt guilty now, and most of all, I didn't want my sorrow to bring him back, to make him sad in any way if he was aware of it. I just couldn't help myself sometimes. I sighed, walked around to the front of the couch, and sat back down between Bo Bo on one pillow and the remote on the other. After another minute of gathering myself, I reached to my right and pressed the button to unmute *The Exorcist*—but suddenly a new movie was starting! I was puzzled, because I knew *The Exorcist* wasn't half over. I watched the new title come up. *Batman Returns*, so I checked the channel—and it had been changed! But I hadn't touched it, I hadn't even been near it! And then I knew beyond a shadow of a doubt, James had just given me a sign. Because James *was* Batman when he was little…

My cousin Joyce had made James a meticulously re-created batman suit for Halloween when he was six. He wore it almost every day until he finally outgrew it. He spent his days jumping off any tall prominence available, yelling "I'm Batman" at regular intervals—until we thought we'd go crazy! Like all kids do, when I tried to warn him about strangers, he'd say, "I'm Batman, I'll karate chop them," while going into a stance with one hand raised to do the chopping. Long after James outgrew the suit, he still loved to become characters at all times of the year, especially Halloween.

When he was older, James sometimes made plans without accounting for the harsher realities of life. He was a dreamer and an optimist, which we loved. With some of his more extreme plans, though, my husband and I would look at each other and say, "I'm Batman," when hearing his latest scheme. He'd laugh along with us, knowing we loved and accepted him, but recognizing that maybe he'd need to rethink whatever he'd just explained, as it might be a little unrealistic. "I'm Batman" became one of our private family jokes. James had loved that movie, and somehow, I think he changed the channel in direct response to my plea to come back, just to let me know I'd see him again. To let me know we *do* go on. *I get it, James. Thank you. Yeah. Batman Returns indeed…*

———

The times that concern me most when James returns are those in which I worry he isn't at peace. But one story made me smile and gave me no doubt that at least some of the time, he was doing just fine. I'd heard some rumors from James's friends, about something that had happened to James's former girlfriend, Regan. So I emailed her and she told me the story herself.

Regan and her sister had taken her sister's little boy with them into the pizza shop where James had been assistant manager. Regan's little nephew was three and was too young to remember James when he was alive. After they finished eating, Regan's sister mentioned that she'd never been to the pizza shop before, adding that the pizza was really good. The child piped in with, "The dead guy likes it a lot." Regan and her sister just stared at each other, knowing perfectly well that James, with his wry sense of humor, would've jokingly described himself just that way to the little boy. Was he standing there in the pizza shop, talking to the child? They both got goosebumps over it.

14

BEST FRIENDS FOR LIFE— AND AFTER

The loss of any young person's life is cause for grief. I met a young woman who came to one of my haunted tea parties, and she told me the story of her best friend.

Emma had been a fun-loving teenage girl who'd never really dealt with losing a loved one. She had watched her friends lose parents and grandparents, seen their grief, and tried her best to comfort them. But she couldn't imagine what that kind of pain felt like. Emma's grandpa had died before she was born, and so had her great-grandparents. This all changed the summer before Emma's freshman year, when she was fourteen.

Emma and her small group of friends were determined to make that summer a great one. They spent nearly every waking moment together, enjoying their lives as only fourteen-year-olds can. Emma and her friends were very close, almost like sisters. But one of her friends was truly special.

Haley was beautiful and smart, with a sense of humor that kept them all laughing. She never wanted to have regrets, which led to taking a few chances. Haley believed that every choice you made was exactly what you wanted to do at that moment. Emma and Haley had a blast that summer.

Emma broke some of her parents' rules and ended up grounded in late August. She remembers Haley calling her to hang out, but Emma had to remind Haley that she was still grounded until the following day. So the best friends made plans to get together then. They talked on for a while and finally hung up, but not before telling each other, "I love you."

Emma was awakened very early the next morning by the worst phone call of her life.

A friend's voice asked her if she'd heard the news. Still half-asleep, Emma said she hadn't heard anything.

"Haley was in a terrible car accident last night, and she didn't make it."

Emma screamed at her friend, telling her it was a sick joke to even say something like that, but her friend insisted it was true. Emma couldn't breathe, and tears poured down her cheeks. Her beautiful friend was dead. And now she knew how all the others had felt when they'd lost someone. She was devastated.

Emma still has vague memories of the calling hours and the funeral service, but not of what occurred there. She realizes now that she was probably still in shock at the time. All Emma's mind could do was keep repeating every scene she had shared with Haley, every memory. She does remember how hard Haley's father hugged her after the funeral, as though he were still hugging his precious daughter.

Emma's mind began to clear when Haley's father asked her and Haley's other friends if they would like to stay at the house with him and Haley's little brother for a week, so they wouldn't be alone. Just so the transition to life without Haley would be a little easier for the family.

After the funeral, at Haley's house, her dad let her friends go into her room and each pick something that would be special to them to keep their memory of Haley alive. Emma picked Haley's favorite horseshoe necklace—she was surprised to find it there because Haley never took it off. Haley called it her good luck charm.

Later on that night, all her friends and Haley's family were sitting in the living room, telling stories about her and how she'd impacted their lives. It was obvious what a great person she'd been. Haley's little brother suddenly said he was hungry, and Emma went to the kitchen to make him something to eat. Haley's house and kitchen were as familiar as her own, and Emma was comfortable taking on the task of fixing a snack.

As Emma opened the freezer and grabbed a bag of pizza rolls, which also happened to be Haley's favorite food, she heard a familiar laugh behind her. It was unmistakable. Haley had the kind of laugh you could never forget.

Emma spun around to find Haley standing beside the sink with an ear-to-ear grin on her face. And as fast as Haley had appeared, she was suddenly gone. Emma, in shock, stood there crying in disbelief that Haley had appeared to her. She hadn't even realized she was crying when a few moments later, Haley's dad came in the kitchen. Haley's dad asked if she was okay. Emma told him what had just happened, and tears began to stream down his face too. There was not an ounce of disbelief in him. He believed his daughter had returned, and he was grateful.

In those few moments that Haley stood there smiling at her best friend, Emma got the closure she needed. Emma knew Haley was okay. She stayed at Haley's house for a week, thinking that maybe she would come back again, that maybe if she stayed there, Haley wouldn't leave.

Finally, she realized Haley was truly gone. But Emma also realized the specialness of Haley having returned from beyond to show her she was happy in her new place. Emma knew she was fortunate to experience Haley's return. Emma only wishes she would have spoken. She wishes she would've told Haley she loved her and that she'd see her again. But Emma thinks Haley already knows this.

"Have you heard from Goo anymore?" I asked my cousin Joyce the next time I saw her. Joyce had called me not long after they lost their lovable old pet terrier. The small dog finally had to be put down at sixteen years of age. They'd grown very close to the little canine family member. Joyce and her husband had inherited the dog after the death of her mother-in-law. The small terrier had become overweight and inactive living with an elderly woman. But when Goo moved to Joyce's house, she lost weight, became active again, and was a huge part of their family for nearly a decade. It was obvious to everyone that Goo loved her new life with Joyce. And the dog's death was hard on them all.

Joyce's family mourned the loss of their little canine member the first weekend after she died. But by the beginning of the following week, something strange began to happen. Still unused to Goo being gone, Joyce was working in her art studio downstairs when she heard Goo get up from her bed just above her and begin shaking her fur. Then came the sound of her toenails moving across the tile floor. This sound had been so common for so many years, and considered so normal in Joyce's everyday routine, that at first, it didn't register. When it did, Joyce stopped what she was doing and listened. Then the toenails stopped.

Joyce's husband, Murphy, a total skeptic most of the time but an avid watcher of the ghost-investigation shows just in case, was still waiting to be convinced of the paranormal. Joyce mentioned what she'd heard to him later that night.

"Oh, I'm sure it was just the tiles creaking or something," he said. And then he heard it for himself! The next day they were both standing downstairs in Joyce's studio while Joyce was busy with doll construction. Joyce's husband gazed out at the backyard and thought about mowing. Suddenly the sound of toenails and a very familiar snort came from upstairs. Murphy looked over at Joyce. "Did you hear that?" Joyce just nodded. They discussed the noises of Goo quietly, noises they couldn't possibly be hearing. Yet they were. They heard Goo's tiny spirit for several more months until the sounds grew fainter and fainter, and further apart. And now Joyce's husband is a bit more of a believer.

Joyce also discovered they weren't the only ones to experience this. A mutual friend of ours would often see her dog after it passed away. The dog was always spotted in his favorite place behind the chair. The pet also had a way of shaking his head, due to his ear problems, and you could hear his ears flap when he did this. His death didn't stop this sound. Our friend heard this distinctive sound a lot in the year or so after her dog died.

————

While interviewing another friend, Teri, at her house, one of her cats jumped up into my lap, and I commented on her pets. Two more felines were winding themselves around my legs and basking in my attention. Teri told me she had a couple cats that were still there, years after they'd died! One of Teri's ghost cats sits outside the door to her room upstairs, and another she had for almost nineteen years still jumps up on her bed. Teri and her husband feel the cat do this all the time. One night not long ago, Teri's husband was already in bed with the light off, and she was in the bathroom. Teri's living cats had followed her, as they usually do, into the bathroom. When she came into the bedroom, her husband asked which cat was in there with *him*. Teri answered that none of them were—that they'd all been with her in the bathroom.

"I felt a cat jump on the bed, and its tail brushed my back!" Teri's husband insisted. Teri said her husband sleeps facing the door, and he can often see the shape of a cat sitting there waiting for his wife. But the moment Teri touches the doorknob to come to bed, the cat disappears. She believes this is her old cat Ditsy, and Teri still has a picture of that room, with this cat in it—taken four years after the cat died.

Apparently even our dogs and cats can stick around for a while, according to these and other stories I've heard. It leaves you in wonder over the possibilities. Animals do not know about heaven or hell, and yet even their spirits stay with us. It certainly gives food for thought, or maybe re-thought, would be the better word. Rethinking all the religious stuff we've been taught from childhood is something I've been doing my entire life—because of ghosts!

15

PLAYING HANGMAN

Many paranormal investigators begin their interest in the paranormal as children, and in that regard, Brian Fain of Massillon Ghost Hunters Society is no different. But what makes Brian's lifelong interest in spirits from the tender age of five so unique is that *his* grandpa drew him a picture from the grave! Brian's memory of one particular summer day forms the basis for what happened a few months later.

Brian was sitting at the table on his grandpa's knee, with his mom and dad seated across from them. The adults were all talking, and Brian's grandpa doodled as he talked. Brian's grandpa had always had a habit of doodling, and he only doodled one specific thing—stick figures. Anytime his grandfather was talking, he was drawing these figures; it was just his thing. Brian recalls playing with something on the table in front of him while he listened to the adults conversing. He also remembers a small notepad in front of his grandpa, and it was covered with the stick figures.

In October of that year, Brian's grandpa passed away in his sleep of a heart attack. Brian, being so young, didn't really understand the nature of death, but of course his parents did, and they grieved. Two months later, it was Christmas, and Santa brought little Brian one of those children's double-sided easels. A pair of small chairs came with the easel, and you could sit and draw with chalk on either side. Brian the five-year-old was ecstatic. He watched as his dad assembled it, putting together the easel itself, and then each little chair. The last thing his father did was tear open the plastic bag of chalk and lay the pieces in the concave tray at the bottom of the easel. Brian wanted to draw on the easel right away, but as soon as he moved toward it, his dad spoke.

"No, no, Brian, we have to go to your other grandparents' house and see what presents Santa left for you there! As soon as we get back, though, you can come try this out." With a frown and a backward glance at the untouched chalkboard, Brian, with the typical impatience of a five-year-old, was led grumpily away by one small hand.

After a full day of opening presents at the home of his mother's parents, eating dinner, and then visiting with his cousins and relatives, Brian's parents finally brought him home that evening. As tired as he was, the Christmas present his dad had assembled that morning was uppermost in his mind. Brian immediately ran downstairs to his basement playroom to draw on the untouched chalkboard—he really wanted to be the first one to do so.

Moments later, Brian's parents heard him yelling and screaming at the top of his young lungs. They came on the run, thinking he had hurt himself, and his dad rounded the corner first.

"Brian, what's wrong? Are you okay?" asked his dad.

"You drew on the chalkboard!" Brian yelled, stomping one foot angrily. "I wanted to be the first one!"

"No, Brian, I didn't draw on it, remember? I just put it together, and then we all left for your other grandma's."

Puzzled, Brian's father came closer, just as Brian's mom entered the room. Both parents could see that something was drawn on the board. Brian's father stared, shocked at what he saw. A large stick figure, at least five inches tall and five inches wide, was drawn on the chalkboard. It was exactly like the stick figures his recently deceased father always drew.

Brian remembers his mother and father exchanging a long glance, but he didn't grasp the full significance at age five. Later on, when he was a little older, Brian remembered his grandpa's drawings and realized what had happened—his grandpa had come back to him. Brian believed it was his grandpa's way of saying Merry Christmas.

For the next several years that Brian played with the chalkboard, he maintained a routine. He would draw upon it, then wipe away his artwork with the small eraser that came with the set. But he noticed he could never completely wipe away his grandpa's stick figure—there was always a shadow of it left on the chalkboard. Even though nothing else Brian drew left a mark when *it* was erased, the shadow of the stick figure always remained, as if it were somehow burned upon the chalkboard's surface. This one incident caused Brian to believe in the unseen, and as he grew older, he began to check out library books about ghosts.

Four years later when he was nine, Brian stayed at his other grandparents' house, and since they lived between two cemeteries, he remembers wondering if ghosts could walk through his grandparents' home from one cemetery to get to the cemetery on the other side to see their friends. Brian had a little tape recorder, and he tried to capture noises or voices of ghosts talking—an early precursor to EVPs (electronic voice phenomena)—but he never recorded any spirits walking through his grandparents' house. I can't even imagine what might've happened if he had!

Life intruded after that, so years went by before Brian decided to hunt for ghosts again. He saw a TV show that used a tape recorder to pick up EVPs and suddenly realized he'd been doing the same thing at age nine! So Brian asked his wife if she minded if he bought a recorder, and after she got over the shock of him explaining he wanted to record dead people, Brian jumped right in and hasn't stopped since.

Brian's family members became involved in his efforts early on, and several of them had already had their own ghostly experiences. Brian's brother-in-law was very familiar with a haunting in the first house built in Upshur County, West Virginia, the Daniel Farnsworth log home, built in 1818.

When the Civil War came, the owners of the home decided that rather than get shot up by soldiers on both sides of the conflict, they'd turn the house into a bed-and-breakfast type of establishment, serving food to officers and allowing them to stay there. This took place mostly while the troops were going to and from the front lines. The officers would sleep in the upstairs of the home and the troops would camp out on and around the grounds. Many times, the wounded, the dying, and even the dead, were carried to the home directly from the battlefield.

When Brian's brother-in-law was young, his aunt owned the house. As a teen, he would stay often at his aunt's house, and sometimes when he came down in the morning to make himself breakfast, all the cabinets would be open. He would close them and go to work, but when he got home, they'd all be open again. Sometimes the drawers were open too. This happened regularly. Years later as an adult, he and his wife lived in the house again. One time his wife was shocked to see a scene materialize before her in one of the rooms—Abraham Lincoln playing checkers with a general. It was as clear and present as anything else in the room, then suddenly it was gone.

Brian's sister-in-law felt very silly even mentioning this to anyone, but it was too incredible not to tell.

Who knows whether this was possible, but Old Abe *did* travel around to meet his generals—and he also played checkers. It's just possible, though unable to be confirmed, that Abe might have come there while traveling to meet with his command.

The aunt eventually rented out the old home but could not keep renters because of the hauntings. Tenants would sign a year's lease and then be gone in six months. Finally his aunt decided to make it a six-month lease instead, but still couldn't keep renters beyond that. Finally, the house sat empty for a long time, and Brian's group, MGHS, was invited to investigate.

Brian had tried to rig up his laptop as a way to listen to EVPs in real time to better communicate with whatever resided there, but after trying it for about twenty seconds, he realized it wasn't working. He then shut off the recorder. When MGHS later played back those twenty seconds, Brian had asked, "What is your name?" And a man's voice answers, "Daniel," which is great evidence, considering the man who built the home was named Daniel.

Later, while they were all downstairs, they heard boots walking across the floor upstairs. Then they heard the low tones of conversation. When the group members followed, the footsteps moved to the second floor, always walking away from Brian as he neared. He literally followed the footsteps all over the house.

Brian hadn't had time to do a full spirit profile on the old house before they were invited to investigate it. This is what most ghost hunters do, and it includes land and record searches to find who built and lived at a house. When Brian found out that Daniel Farnsworth was the builder, he realized his twenty-second EVP had probably caught the voice of the original owner. But the jury is still out on the vision of Abraham Lincoln!

16

BUMPS IN THE NIGHT

Pandora's home was a historic one built in the last century on a very old trail called the Carolina Road, which had been traveled by everyone since the area was first settled in the 1700s. In fact, the trail was used long before that by traders and Native Americans. Pandora's house was once a place where people could stop and stay, or even purchase a few goods before continuing on their way. Eventually, it was turned into a private home, and Pandora and her husband have lived there for almost a decade. Many historic homes surrounded Pandora's house as well. The neighborhood buildings run the gamut from schools to plantations. The one thing they have in common is that all of them are old.

The phone rang one day, and it was my artist friend Pandora, calling from her home in a Southern state six hours away.

I had just spoken to her a few days before, as she told me her ghost stories and wondered if she'd forgotten something.

"Oh my God. I'm shaking! My sewing machine just started running without me!"

I didn't understand what she meant, and Pandora explained.

She'd come into her workroom and had sat down not two feet away, when the machine began sewing by itself. Pandora knew the machine could only run by the foot pedal, so there was no way this could be happening. It really freaked her out, and she thought maybe one of her cats had snuck in and stepped on the pedal. But when she checked, there were no cats in the room with her.

We talked for a little while, and I thanked her for telling me about it. She'd told me many stories of the unseen residents of her home when we'd talked earlier that week, and I knew it was just another normal day in her haunted house. She still loved her home and had grown as used to the spirits as she could. The ghosts continued to present themselves in different ways, so there was never a dull moment. The phenomena hadn't really lessened over the years either.

About the third week after Pandora and her husband had moved into their home a decade earlier, Pan began to hear singing between the hours of 2:00 and 4:00 a.m., and it usually woke her up. It was very soft, but obviously a woman. It sounded like a lilting, almost Gaelic song to Pandora. And as soon as she heard the singing each time, the house would go cold.

One day, not long after this started, a man stopped by who knew the area well and was related to most of the town's founders. Pandora decided to bring up the singing and was surprised to be told she'd heard the voice of Mary.

"Mary? Are you telling me this place is haunted?" Pandora asked apprehensively.

"No worse than any of these other buildings on this section of land. It's the land itself that's haunted," said the old man, chuckling a bit. Then he proceeded to tell Pandora about her ghost.

Mary was a medicine woman who used to travel around with her herbs and potions, riding on the back of a white mule. She was found dead one day near what is now Pandora's property, and she just sort of stayed around. The man told Pan she was very lucky to hear her, though, as not very many people did. He was of the opinion that this meant Mary really liked Pandora.

"Oh, goodie for me," Pan told him sarcastically. "Maybe I can get a discount or something for buying a haunted house!"

A few weeks after that, Pandora's son-in-law was fetching something in her bedroom, where Pan kept a small wooden box with a lid on her dresser. Her son-in-law came out white-faced a few moments afterward.

He'd just watched the lid come off the box and move across the dresser!

Soon after, both Pan's son-in-law and daughter felt the room they were in go cold, and then *they* heard Mary singing too. In a way, Pandora was glad, since it was no longer just her who'd experienced it now.

The front bedroom in Pandora's house is also freezing. It stays cold all the time, not just intermittently, and there is a lot of activity there too. Pandora only has one cat that will even go in the front room. But the front bedroom is certainly not the only haunted place in the house. Pandora told me another story, one that had truly scared her.

About three years earlier, Pandora was doing the laundry. Her washer and dryer were in the hallway near that very cold front bedroom. No one else was home at the time. Pan suddenly felt a slight pressure on her left shoulder, and then someone whispered in her ear! She could feel their breath on her face—it even moved her hair. It was a woman's voice with an almost Irish brogue-type lilt. "I'm watching you," said the voice.

The voice wasn't sinister at all; it was more like a matter-of-fact statement—as if she was just telling Pan that she was watching her do the laundry.

I told Pandora that the ghost might not know what a washing machine was, and Pan agreed.

But either way, Pan almost fainted. Her knees buckled, and she just about went down. Pandora thought this reaction may have scared the spirit because she didn't hear singing, or much of anything else, for a good year and a half. And that was a relief.

I asked if the house had ever been investigated by a paranormal team, and Pandora said it had. She'd met a professor of parapsychology at one of her art shows. She and Pan got to talking, and the lady mentioned the trail that Pan lived on. Pan told her that she thought her house was haunted, and the professor asked if it was okay to bring a crew to see what they could pick up.

Not long after, the lady and her team showed up with lots of gadgets and electronics and went through the house and all around the property outside. Finally they came back inside and told Pandora the house wasn't haunted, rather it was the ground itself, just as the old man had originally told her. The professor said there was so much activity outside she couldn't believe it.

Pandora's neighbor eventually told her they heard the singing in their house too, so the ghost definitely doesn't just stay in one place. The ghost of Mary comes and goes on the haunted ground. Pan believes she must've upset the ghost badly when she almost fainted that day doing laundry, and maybe the spirit went over to the neighbors for a while.

I told Pandora no one could fault her for nearly passing out. Even seasoned professionals still get frightened by direct contact.

Pandora said that when she and her husband sit in their living room, they can see shadows. They appear and disappear with no rhyme or reason, nor is there anything that could be making a shadow. A lot of the time, along with the shadows, they will smell a rose scent, and sometimes cigarette smoke—and neither of them smoke.

I wondered aloud whether Mary brought the rose scent when she appeared.

Then Pan told me that just the other day she'd had the exterminator out to inspect, and they were talking about the age of her home. He was standing in front of the sink facing Pan's living room, and Pan was facing him. All of a sudden, every ounce of color went out of this poor man's face—at something behind Pan! She turned around quickly to see a shadow moving down the wall toward the bedroom. It passed over a quilt she had hanging there, which made it even more obvious. The exterminator said, "Did you see that?"

"Yeah, it happens all the time around here," Pan told him.

"I've gotta go," he said abruptly. And he got out of there fast.

It was a very dark shadow, according to Pandora, and really tall and thin. She hadn't seen where it came from, and the guy didn't stick around to tell her. The shadow had touched the ceiling but didn't come all the way down to the floor. It was almost as though someone was walking down the hall but their feet weren't touching the ground. The shadow just continued on down and into the bedroom. After the exterminator walked out, Pandora went into the bedroom herself to check it out. The room was ice cold, so she knew something had been there. All Pandora had to say was, "I bet I won't get that guy back to spray for bugs!"

Pan then told me her son-in-law dreads having to stay in that front bedroom when they visit. But Pan sleeps there now, mostly to get away from her husband's snoring, and she's okay with that because she just knows it's not something that's going to hurt her. It sometimes just feels to Pandora as if they are in a different dimension, functioning as they used to and not even aware of them.

"That's what we call a residual haunting, recurring over and over but unaware of you. Now, Mary, or whoever it was who whispered to you in your laundry room, that would be classified as an intelligent haunting—a spirit who can interact with you," I told her.

Pan said her daughter, son-in-law, and their two young sons came to stay over the Christmas holidays. One of their kids had a cold, so Pan's daughter got up and went into the front room to rock him. Pan said that when anyone walks across the floor in the front room, there is a distinctive creaking, and everything vibrates. Her daughter was rocking away and suddenly felt the vibrations behind her. She thought her father had gotten up and maybe was using the bathroom. She said, "Hey, Pops, what are you doing up?" But there was no answer. Suddenly, Pan's daughter heard the sound of many feet beginning to march in formation, passing by her. She could feel the wind from them moving past, and they continued on by her and right on out the front door! Her daughter froze in fear for a moment, but then felt it wasn't anything that would do them harm, so she was able to relax and resume rocking her child.

This incredible story made sense. The area was involved in both the Revolutionary War and the Civil War, so troops marching there would've been common during those times.

The next night, Pandora's daughter was out in the front room again, around the same time in the early morning, and the same thing happened. Not too long after that, a friend of Pandora's, a nurse, came to stay with Pan after she had surgery. Pandora was only comfortable sleeping in the recliner, so her friend slept in the living room with her. The marching woke Pan's friend up one night, while Pandora had been lying there awake. Pandora felt the wind go past, but thought it was from the heavy meds they'd given her after her operation. But Pan's friend confirmed that it wasn't the meds! Later, Pandora found out they used to march the Revolutionary War prisoners right through there on their way to the town north of them. This sound and the vibration of the troops passing by, along with the wind, is really something to witness. Pandora said it lasts for quite a few seconds each time it happens.

I mentioned residual hauntings again, the kind that play the same scene over and over like a tape loop. This was what the marching seemed to be. But the ghost of Mary singing and whispering in her ear, that was definitely intelligent, able to interact with the living and make herself understood. The shadow could have been either of those, but without further investigation, it is hard to speculate.

I thanked Pandora for calling to fill me in on the sewing machine running by itself, and I joked that perhaps Mary was learning how to operate twenty-first-century machinery. Maybe after observing how great the modern washer was, Mary was ready to try the sewing machine too!

17

DÉJÀ VU

My next-door neighbor called, and I could tell right away she was excited about something.

"Your book!" blurted Tammy. "I just read the part about the ghost in the red plaid shirt! I've seen him too!"

It didn't hit me right away what she was talking about. My first book had just shipped to all those who'd ordered it before its upcoming release. I'd already been hearing back from friends and acquaintances who'd received their copy.

Tammy was talking about a section where I'd recounted many of the paranormal events in my haunted house. One night while sitting on the sofa reading a book in my front room, I'd felt someone watching me. I looked up, over toward the living room, and saw a young man with long, dark hair standing silently beside the fireplace, staring at me. He simply stood, hands at his sides, wearing a red plaid shirt with black suspenders and dark pants. I couldn't see the fireplace through him, so he looked as solid and as real as anyone. Shocked and caught off guard, I squealed and looked away, then looked back. And just like that, he was gone. I've never seen him again, but I've speculated he was the former owner or possibly the owner's son.

My neighbor Tammy told me that during their first year there, she saw the same man constantly. He always walked across the breezeway at the back of their house, then crossed over into our garage! When her two boys began having nightmares, Tammy finally had a guy come and do a cleansing in her basement, the part of their house that felt the creepiest to Tammy and her family.

Tammy and I had lived beside each other for thirteen years but had only recently begun to walk together in the evenings. She'd never told me this story about the man before. I suddenly realized he might be related to someone in their house. Tammy's home was the original Victorian house on this tract of land, and we were once told that *our* home had been built beside it for a family member. If this is true, the man in the red plaid shirt probably felt comfortable in either house. He may have crossed back and forth often to visit his parents or whoever lived in the older Victorian house. Tammy and I speculated on different scenarios for a while, but of course we still don't know for sure. The research I've done is inconclusive. I only know that each of us banished our spirits into other areas in our respective houses—away from us!

18

HOUSE-GHOSTS

My friend Teri has coexisted with something in her home for many years. The village where Teri lives is picturesque, with a quaint main street crowded with small shops and Gothic churches. I drove through the small town and pulled up in front of her home. Teri was just a few months old when her parents moved their family to the century-old brick house tucked between two downtown buildings.

As I stepped onto the red-brick front porch, I admired the iron Victorian gate, which along with the arched windows, gave away the home's age. Teri answered the door, a big smile lighting up her pretty face, and ushered me inside. A long, steep staircase climbed the wall just inside to the left, instantly giving off a vibe of something up there. I glanced up at it and immediately made a mental note to ask what happened on these stairs, or at the top of them, as the psychic feeling coming from them was pretty intense.

We walked through the house and sat at the kitchen table, Teri's friendly cats checking me out the entire time, and Teri began to tell me about her haunted house.

Almost as far back as she can remember, Teri recalls seeing perfectly round balls of light zipping around the hallway outside her bedroom, which was just up those stairs inside the front door. They were about the size of tennis balls, very brightly colored, and hovered and darted through the hall. Teri remembers as a child being fascinated with the balls of light. Later on, when she was still a little girl, Teri would go into the basement and hold long conversations with someone. Her mother would come down to bring her upstairs, but Teri loved her talks and tea parties with the man she called "Old MacDonald."

Later in her adult life, Teri inherited the home from her parents and brought her own small children along.

One night when her daughter was about three, Teri put her to bed and was sitting with her husband on the downstairs sofa with the baby monitor near them. They began to hear their daughter talking from her upstairs room—and then something began to answer her.

Teri ran up to her daughter's room and found her sitting in her closet, deep in conversation with this someone. Teri put her daughter back in bed and tucked her in. Almost as soon as Teri returned to the sofa, their daughter could once again be heard speaking on the baby monitor

—in a conversation with someone! Her tiny daughter would talk, and then a strange voice would answer her. Teri ran back upstairs, and once again, her little girl was sitting in the closet, engrossed in a visit with someone only she could see. This brought back Teri's childhood memories of "Old MacDonald," her basement friend.

One night, Teri was giving her girls a bath before she put them to bed. When she'd tucked them in, she came down the front stairs and into the living room. Teri's husband suddenly asked, "What did you need earlier?" Puzzled, Teri told him she hadn't needed anything.

Teri told her husband she hadn't come down. He just shook his head. "Then I can tell you for sure that one of our ghosts has blond hair!" He'd been sitting on the sofa when someone with blond hair stuck her head around the corner, as if to ask him the location of something. Then whoever it was left again, as though they'd suddenly remembered where it was. But Teri had been busy bathing the girls and hadn't moved from the bathroom.

Teri told me it is common for them to hear footsteps that go up and down the hall upstairs when no one is up there. They hear the doors open and close sometimes. The dogs and cats freak out about this; it's obvious they can hear and see something that Teri and her husband can't! Then the footsteps usually descend the stairs, but that's all they do. Teri always assumed whoever it was was going out the front door, and maybe that's why the footfalls stopped there.

One day Teri was in the bathroom just off the kitchen and her husband was in the next room when she heard the back door open. Teri pointed behind me toward the back door to show me how close it was. Teri and I were seated at her kitchen table, just a few feet from the bathroom. The living room was beyond it, around the corner from where we sat at the kitchen table.

Their dogs heard the back door open too, and they came thundering through the house to see who it was. Teri heard a female voice yell, "Hey," so she finished up quickly and hurried out of the bathroom, thinking it was their older daughter. Teri didn't see anyone, so she went to the living room to ask her husband what their daughter had wanted.

Teri's husband told her their daughter wasn't there—that no one had been there. But he told Teri he too had heard the back door open and the voice call out. They were both dumbfounded. It took them a while to get over that one!

One day, when their girls were a little older, about five and seven, they were having a huge fight in their room. After arguing back and forth as sisters sometimes do, they came running to Teri suddenly, very scared. In the middle of their argument, a stuffed animal had come flying into their room from the hallway, as though someone had thrown it at them—as if someone was angrily saying, "Knock it off!" The girls were the only ones upstairs that day. Yet the girls seemed to know it wasn't a malicious act; it was more as if someone had become annoyed at their bickering and wanted them to shut up!

Teri's father had been a carpenter, and their garage had been his workshop. He always told everyone who came into his shop with a lit cigarette to put it out because the sawdust in the air could spark. This is how Teri's dad taught them to never smoke around woodworking. Teri and her husband had recently been involved in restoring the house, and one night Teri needed to cut a board, which she'd learned to do herself. She walked into the garage with a lit cigarette and laid it down on the lip of the saw. When she turned back around to get it, someone had stubbed it out. Teri just knew that was her dad.

I asked Teri how her husband reacted to all this ghostly stuff. "He takes it in stride, mostly because he's had his own experiences," she told me. Teri's husband has an old rocking chair upstairs that had belonged to his grandma. When he was in college, this rocker was in his dorm. One night he woke up to go to the bathroom, and the chair was rocking. He thought he could see a form sitting in it, but since he was half-asleep, he sort of blew it off. By the time he got back to his room, he was wide awake, and now he could see for certain that it was his grandma, sitting there in the chair, rocking! Teri's husband stuck out his hand, wanting to try to touch his grandma, and his hand felt like it went through a cold mist, and then suddenly she was gone; she dissolved, just like that.

Teri taught her girls that they should ask one of the ghosts, who they nicknamed "Gertie," to bring back anything the girls couldn't find, the items that went missing. One time, her younger daughter lost her favorite bouncy ball. It was just a small ball, but the little girl loved it. She asked Gertie out loud to find it and bring it to her, and later that day, while she was sitting on the floor watching TV, the ball suddenly appeared beside her on the floor. This would be known as an "apport," where a spirit can make objects appear out of thin air or move items from one area to another.

Teri and her extended family live peacefully with their spirits these days. As I finished up our interview and said my goodbyes, I made my way through the iron gate again, giving a backward glance up at the old brick house as I walked back to my car on the street. I had the sense of many eyes watching me go.

19

SHARED TRAGEDY

I met a woman a few years ago at one of my favorite music venues, and through our shared tragedy—the untimely deaths of our young adult sons—we bonded. Over the years since my own son James's death, Sandy and I have become good friends. Sandy encouraged me in my new writing career, and we talked often about our sons, the spirit world, and the returns of loved ones. She finally told me about some of her own son's returns.

Her son Tim was only twenty-one when he died suddenly of a brain aneurysm. Obviously, this was a terribly traumatic time for her. And just as with James, neither Sandy nor I got to say goodbye.

Over the years since Tim died, Sandy has had a few experiences with him returning to her. Amazingly, Tim and James were very much alike; Sandy and I believe they would have been friends if they had ever met. Tim was full of excitement and drive, focused on whatever thing held the top slot of his interest at any given time. He wouldn't rest until he'd conquered it or mastered it—whether it was skateboarding, motorcycling, getting something he wanted, or achieving some level of mastery over a particular subject. James was the very same way. At some point, to his friends Tim became synonymous with a star symbol. Sandy believes it was from a logo on his motorcycle. James, a professional rollerblader and musician, developed a broken heart symbol, which stood for his extreme rollerblading crew, The Jolly, Jolly Heartbreakers. One day, Tim came home with an open star tattooed on the back of his neck, shaded with lime green, his favorite color. (James came home one day with the broken heart tattoo on the side of *his* neck.) After their deaths, all their friends each got Tim's and James's distinctive tattoos. The similarities between our sons are uncanny. Sandy told me a strange story about the star.

One day at work on her lunch hour, Sandy's left hand started hurting. It felt like a bruise and when she looked, there was a bump right below her ring finger. She didn't remember hitting it on anything and couldn't figure out what caused the discomfort. She went back to work and about an hour later, she just happened to look down at her hand. There was a perfectly shaped star where the bump had been! The blue bruise beneath the skin was shaped like a star—her son's signature mark. Without saying anything about what *she* thought it looked like, Sandy asked five people at work if they saw anything on her hand. Without any hesitation at all, they confirmed it was a star. Later Sandy took a picture of it to show her husband in case it started to fade away. Sandy just knew somehow that it was Tim letting her know he was with her.

Sandy also told me she gets a feeling of urgency sometimes when sitting on their sofa facing the door to her hallway. Usually, she's reading or doing a crossword puzzle, when she feels an intense need to look up. As soon as she does, near the top of the wall is a cloud of white fog, which quickly passes by. Her eyes follow the solid wall between the two doorways to see if the white cloud exits on the other side, but it never does. It's as though it just disappears. But along with the white cloud, Sandy feels Tim's presence very strongly each time. She believes it's Tim, maybe coming to check out his room. Sandy thinks he also wants to let her know he's still there with her. Each time Sandy has seen the white cloud, it only lasts a few seconds, but it's enough to leave her with a strong sense of peace and comfort.

Sandy told me that a few years earlier, they'd put in a new kitchen floor. While they'd been talking with the floor installer about the kitchen, they'd asked him about doing the same thing in their bathroom. The installer told them he had a scrap piece of flooring in his truck that they could have, and she and her husband could just pay for installation. Since their bathroom was very small, the piece of flooring would work just fine.

They all decided the installer would come another day to put down the bathroom floor. The day he came, Sandy was at work, but her husband was home to take care of things. When the installer showed up, he told Sandy's husband he had a different scrap piece they could look at, then decide which one they wanted to use. This new piece was darker than the first one, with squares in shades of browns and creams. Sandy's husband called her for her opinion, and she told him whichever one he decided upon would be fine with her. Sandy's husband picked the new piece.

About a week later, Sandy noticed a perfect letter T—the first initial of their son Tim's name—on one of the squares. Sandy remembered that they'd never seen the flooring before the day the installer offered it to them. She decided to take a picture of the tile. The most amazing part to Sandy is that on the same square with the letter T, there is a face—and it is the face of her son, Tim. Without a shadow of a doubt, it is his face. Sandy has the photo that matches the tile exactly. The eyes, nose, mouth, and the unusual haircut Tim had at that time are all represented. Sandy believes it's another sign from Tim. She doesn't understand how these strange things can happen, but they do. Sandy had one more sign from her deceased son.

At the same time they did the flooring, the couple also painted the walls in their entire home. Tim's room was a bright lime green and had been for years. He just loved that color. They'd surprised him one year while he was gone and painted it for him. He never repainted it. Tim had also put many glow-in-the-dark stars on his ceiling in all sizes, from very tiny to quite large. I had to laugh as I told Sandy that James also had these stars on *his* ceiling. Sandy just shook her head at how alike our sons were.

And in addition to the star being Tim's signature mark, bright lime green was also his favorite color, so Sandy never intended to repaint his room—she was just going to leave it as it was. But after they'd painted all the other rooms in the house, there was some paint left over. Sandy's husband said they might as well paint Tim's room because they couldn't leave it like that forever. He reasoned that since it would eventually have to be done, this was as good a time as any. So Sandy went along with the plan, but first, she took every star off the ceiling. It took a long time because she was careful not to get them all over the floor. Sandy made sure she got every one of them. Sandy even saved a few, just to keep. With that done, she and her husband moved on to the walls.

They had to put two coats of primer on the walls just to cover the green. But as they began to do it, Sandy started getting really sick to her stomach. As they got to the last wall of green, she thought she was going to vomit. It had suddenly hit Sandy—the last remnants of her precious son were gone! She started crying hysterically, saying, "What have we done? What have we done?" Sandy's husband tried to comfort her, but she was inconsolable. Sandy cried the whole weekend and just felt really sick. All vestiges of Tim's old room were gone now, the room was freshly painted, and Sandy was emotionally drained.

On the last evening of the weekend, Sandy was stoically cleaning stuff up and getting things ready for work the next day, when she turned off the light in the bedroom. Suddenly Sandy realized there was still a light on in the room. She didn't understand what was going on at first. Sandy even turned the light switch on and off a few times, because she didn't get it. Then Sandy realized her shirt was glowing! She looked down and saw the glow-in-the-dark stars all over it! She hadn't dropped very many, and any that she did, she picked right back up. Tim's old room was completely clean, and the stars were gone. So how did so many get all over Sandy's shirt? To her, this was a final sign from Tim, just letting his mother know that no matter what color his room was, he would always be with her, and she would always feel him around her. This was exactly what Sandy needed to know, right when she needed her son to show her.

I look forward to the day when I can finally go to Sandy's house to see her special bathroom tile. I often wonder about the son who was so much like my own. I hope they've met each other by now, wherever they are. I just know they'd be friends.

20

GET THE BABY

I drove to Amish Country after my friend and fellow investigator Darrin Troyer of the Amish Paranormal Society told me what had happened to a woman he knew. Darrin's friend Lani and her husband own a business in Amish Country. After a few phone calls, I finally scheduled our interview.

I parked across the street from their store and waited in the crosswalk for the light to turn. The town was bustling with tourists visiting the many shops on either side of the street. I had met Lani and her husband the previous October while visiting their store during a Halloween event. The quaint little town had arranged ghost tours at all the participating buildings that supposedly had ghosts. My friend Darrin had set up his group's merchandise and displays on a table at the back of Lani's store. Then Darrin gave a short presentation to the customers who made the rounds of the spooky downtown stores.

Lani's old store held all the ambience of its century-plus years. She greeted me from behind a raised counter made of old wood, which gleamed mellowly under the overhead lights. A pretty, delicately featured woman with dark hair, she smiled at the sight of me walking through the high, wide doors.

I greeted Lani and told her I was glad we could finally find a time to meet. Lani thanked me for not giving up on her, as she had been very busy. Summer tourist season in Amish Country was a sight to behold—you could not tell that anything was wrong with the economy when in Amish Country. People flocked there from throughout Ohio and nearby states. In fact, a rough economy had helped our Amish Country flourish because it is just a short trip away for many, and thus a less expensive adult vacation destination.

Darrin had told me just a little about what had happened to Lani the previous fall.

Lani had been through chemo not long before this event, and her thoughts had turned to what awaits us all after death. A little morbid perhaps, but considering the circumstances, I'm sure many of us would have dealt with the same feelings.

Lani told me she had driven to an old cemetery in Coshocton County and had brought her video camera along. She'd been searching for the graves of some of her husband's relatives. This cemetery was a small one, more or less in the middle of nowhere. There were no houses nearby, and there weren't any cars passing by either. It was very quiet and isolated, at the end of a long dirt road that led back into the graves. But it was a beautiful summer day, and Lani decided to switch on the camera as she walked through the cemetery. As a sort of narration, Lani decided to read off some of the headstones out loud as she passed by while she continued to look for her husband's family surname. Lani started making comments about a few of the stones. Some were decrepit, with chunks missing or huge cracks marring the names of the deceased, and she commented on that sad state of affairs.

Lani then saw several stones of very young children who'd died, one of them just a baby. This was depressing, and she remarked on that too. She kept a running dialogue for a good ten to fifteen minutes until finally, near the back of the cemetery, Lani found her husband's family name. At that point, Lani shut the camera off and studied the headstone information.

Just as Lani got to this point in her story, customers walked through the front doors of her shop and Lani greeted them as they passed us. Lani smiled apologetically at me for the interruption, then turned toward her laptop on the counter, brought up a file, and hooked up a small satellite speaker. "Here, listen for yourself," Lani told me as she fiddled with the computer.

After Lani had returned home from the cemetery trip, she'd downloaded the video and watched it. It was pretty shocking.

Lani started the video, and we both stared at her laptop screen. The first thing I saw was the lush green grass bathed in the full sun of a summer day. The weathered tombstones were brightly lit. Then I heard the sound of Lani's voice begin commenting on the stones as she started her tour through the small cemetery. The trees could be seen in the background with their leaves undulating in a light breeze. A perfect summer day.

Suddenly, I heard something else. Cocking my head to the side, I listened closely, searching Lani's face. She nodded confirmation at what I was now hearing. There was another sound coming from the speaker now—a second intonation—a whispery, paper-thin voice, seemingly ancient with age. It faded in and out, rising above Lani's calm narration, then dropping to nearly inaudible syllables. But as Lani commented on the tombstones of the children and the baby who'd died so young, the raspy voice rose and became clear and distinct. "Get the baby ..." gasped the woman. My mouth nearly dropped open. The sound of Lani talking on pleasantly, obliviously, came from the speaker. So did the strange woman's voice, mumbling something, carrying on a conversation as though she walked right beside Lani, telling her secrets and trying to get her attention. I got the feeling it had been a long time since anyone had been to that cemetery, and the woman was simply conversing with this welcome person who'd happened along. Then suddenly the odd, scratchy voice rose again. "GET THE BABY!" she shouted, very distinctly, as if this demand was of the utmost importance—and as if she wasn't long dead and wasn't trying to save a long-dead baby.

I looked at Lani, amazed, and she nodded and shut the video off as it finished. "Lani, do you realize that paranormal investigators spend thousands of hours just to get a single EVP? Just one significant, clear word, or if they're *very* lucky, a short sentence from a spirit? And you have recorded a fifteen-minute conversation; a class A, clearly articulated, and distinct communication from a spirit? It's unbelievable!"

Lani nodded again and then replayed the video in its entirety. We both watched and listened again in silence, with me shaking my head in awe. It was pretty amazing.

"If only I'd have known she was there," said Lani.

"Did you go back, to see if you could get anything else?" I asked.

"No, I never did," Lani trailed off.

My always-curious investigator antennae were twitching wildly by this point, and I got her to explain exactly where this cemetery was, thinking that maybe I could go with Brian or some of my ghost hunter friends later on. It was truly an amazing piece of video, and I'd never seen anything like it before. A thought struck me, and I asked

Lani if she'd ever had any other experiences like this one. I was thinking maybe Lani was a bit psychic herself and, like most sensitive people, might have attracted this sort of thing.

Lani told me that after her mom died, she was really torn up about it. Her mother had always said if there was a way she could come back and let Lani know something, she would. Right after her mom died, Lani went down to her basement to work on crafts, and she started thinking about her mom. She began to cry a little bit, and spoke out loud to her mother too. And suddenly, the lights switched off and then back on, eight times. She knew how many because she counted it. Lani was able to laugh out loud then and tell her, "Okay, Mom. I know it's you, and I know you're okay."

I told her this had happened to a lot of people I'd talked with. Somehow, sometimes, our loved ones seem able to come back to give us a sign when we need it most.

Lani told me that the only other time she'd really noticed anything like this was in an old cabin they'd lived in for a little while when her kids were younger. Lani's kids hated this place—they said there was an old man upstairs with them! They could smell old-man aftershave, and they were constantly teasing each other about it, saying the old man was gonna get one of them, and that sort of thing. They said their clothes would move around. One time they said the old man picked up a pile of their clothes and put it outside their door in the hallway.

As their mother, Lani didn't know what to believe.

"I'd felt a few odd things myself but was so busy, I didn't pay much attention," Lani told me. Finally, they were ready to move and leave the cabin for good. Just two nights before they moved, Lani talked out loud to the old man her kids said lived there with them.

"We're leaving," Lani told him. "So if you really are here, I just wanted to say goodbye." Lani was alone that night, as her husband was out of town. After she crawled into bed, there was sudden pounding on her bedroom door. It was very loud—so loud it vibrated things in the bedroom. Lani jumped up terrified, then slowly and carefully opened the door. No one was there. The next night was their last night in the cabin. Lani's husband was in bed beside her when the pounding on the door started up again. She'd told her husband what had happened the night before, but he hadn't taken it too seriously. When the pounding started again this night, he jumped up, shocked at how loud it was. The sounds reverberated through the walls and door, shaking everything in their bedroom—it was a huge noise. Lani's husband opened the door, ready for battle, and no one was there. Could this have been the old man letting them know he really *was* there with them? They never knew for sure.

Just then, Lani's husband, Rudy, came into the store, returning from an errand. He had a story to tell me regarding something that had happened to a friend of his.

Rudy's friend was a plainspoken, serious man, who had never previously held beliefs in ghosts or paranormal things. Then one day, something happened while he was babysitting his granddaughter. He and the little girl had been out in the yard with a metal detector earlier that day and had found a few items that were obviously from the past century. The house was older, and many had lived on the land over the years. The young granddaughter was as rowdy as children can be, and she and her grandpa had played together and even gotten down on the floor with a game later that evening.

Rudy's friend realized at some point that he'd lost his cell phone. So he called his cell phone number from his home phone. It rang, and the man discovered that the cell phone was under a living room easy chair, probably lost while he and his granddaughter had been playing on the floor. He hung up his home phone and grabbed the cell phone. But as he picked up his cell, it popped up that he had just received a new voicemail. So the man checked his voicemail on the cell, and it was a voicemail from his landline. Somehow, when he had just called his cell phone, a strange voice had been able to leave him a message!

Rudy's friend was so shocked, he had sent Rudy the message. Rudy had it recorded on his own phone, so he played the message back for me. The shaky, tired voice of an old woman began to speak as Rudy pressed the voice-mail key.

"This craziness has got to stop. It's unwarranted." Then the voice's register dropped lower, almost as if the speed was slowing down or the energy was dissipating. "This craziness has got to stop," said the old woman's voice in a slightly lower register, and then again, even lower: "This craziness has got to stop." This last time, the register had dropped so much lower while also slowing down that it sounded like a horror movie special-effects trick.

It was my turn to be shocked. This was the creepiest thing I had ever heard besides the woman screaming about the baby that Lani had recorded! Rudy swore his friend was not savvy enough to fake this, or to even know much of anything about ghosts. But this cell phone message had upset him badly, and he believed the old woman wanted him to quit digging on the property, as he'd been doing that day with the metal detector. The man also thought maybe the wrestling around with his granddaughter had upset her too. He has been quieter lately, hoping she is appeased.

It was the scariest evidence I'd ever heard.

I thanked Lani and her husband for their stories and headed back home, thinking about what they'd told me on my drive. Maybe her recognition of the old man had finally brought him forth from the kid's room. Or maybe he didn't want the family to leave; maybe the kids didn't really bother him all *that* much. And just maybe, some ghosts and spirits can become attached to their new families.

And as for the old woman who thought the rowdiness was unwarranted—well, I don't even know what to think of that. If spirits do exist here on our plane with us, then surely our antics must annoy them at times. And, as an adult, the older I get, the rowdier children seem! I can see how they must sometimes appear to our unseen visitors, especially when they have to share the same house. And the thought of that is enough to keep me awake, and watchful.

––––––

As a psychic and paranormal investigator, I've heard of so many NDEs (near death experiences) that point to an afterlife as either a good or a bad place. But how can ghosts or spirits be reconciled with this? Could our loved ones' spirits be allowed to visit those of us left behind? Is there a certain window of time where our invisible spirits, our matter/energy, hangs around after death, until we finally dissipate? Could some souls be stuck in a sort of purgatory, an in-between state Catholics believe in? I'd always heard ghosts were those not at rest. But this didn't always seem to be the case. Still, this is exactly what I *didn't* want for my son. But that didn't stop the strange returns of my son's spirit from happening.

I'd done a fair amount of research since James and my dad had died. My father's and James's returns had frightened yet fascinated me—but I didn't know how to help them. I'd never been able to use psychic abilities to help myself, and I'd heard other psychics say the same. I'd gone through hell after James's and Dad's deaths, mostly self-blame, thinking I'd brought about this series of personal tragedies. Then being unable to get any sort of psychic info about my son and father was equally frustrating—when I regularly was able to get this sort of information for others. It was almost too much to bear.

Ever since my early teen years at my parents' haunted house on Fifth Street, I'd always known there was more than just this life, so I was probably a little less shocked than most people might be when James began to return after his death. Still, it was traumatic. You just don't expect visits from beyond from those you loved so dearly.

As a young teen in the haunted house, I'd never quite figured out if it was my use of a Ouija board that let something evil in or if spirits were attracted to my psychic streak. I'd found through research that St. Theresa, a Catholic saint, believed that "with extraordinary gifts, come extraordinary trials." I didn't really want to hear that. In fact, it made me feel sick. My religious upbringing hadn't prepared me for anything like this—not returns of loved ones after death, nor psychic abilities. Some of it fit in, but most of it didn't. I'd always leaned toward being a Christian psychic, but that was also an anachronism. The two just didn't really mesh well, at least not in today's society. But the truth is that people from all religious beliefs and all walks of life have these ghostly experiences happen to them. It's a simple fact.

A friend once told me a story about her relative, a generally unpleasant and violent man with lots of problems. Drug addiction, alcoholism, you name it, he had it. These addictions led him to steal anything that wasn't nailed down—even from family and friends. He sold these stolen items for drug money. This man was also a terrible parent to his young child, who was beaten and neglected on a regular basis, until finally, the child was taken away to live elsewhere.

Then the mean man got sick—and he died on the table in the ER. The doctors were able to revive him, but afterwards, he told an incredible story of his near-death experience. The man said he found himself on a platform in the dark, fighting off demons—horrendous-looking creatures—and they were ripping him to pieces. This man recovered from his near death and never touched drugs or a drop of alcohol again. He became very religious and was grateful for what he considered his second chance. This certainly does give pause for thought. Fear is a great motivator. When nothing else worked to stop the addictions, the fear of these demons did. And apparently it was real enough to this man that it didn't take a twelve-step program to stop the addictions in their tracks.

There are many stories of people experiencing a negative afterlife, and this would certainly make an impression on most of us if it happened. I remember my psychic grandma reaching toward the sky before she died, as though toward something or someone only she could see. My dear uncle, Joyce's dad, within days of his death and right before he lapsed into his final coma, asked Joyce and her mom if they could see that bright light up in the corner. Of course, no one but my uncle could see it—he was about to go *into* that light, and they were not.

An acquaintance told me that his father, after being mute and unresponsive to people and stimuli for years with end-stage Alzheimer's kept staring up at the ceiling on the last day of his life. His father was an atheist; he believed that when you died that was it. He was also an abusive, controlling, and violent disciplinarian, administering regular beatings to his youngest son, whom he seemed to single out. This treatment caused permanent lifelong psychological damage to the boy when he matured, leading him to become abusive himself. The entire family lived in fear of the father's tirades. Eventually the Alzheimer's softened the man's personality somewhat, which helped his son to partially forgive his father for his past abuse.

"Dad, what are you looking at?" the son asked his father. "Are you seeing God, and heaven?" His father turned his head to meet his son's eyes, acknowledging him, as though to say "yes," then went right back to staring intently above him. He hadn't acknowledged his son, or anyone for that matter, for years, due to the disease taking away his ability to recognize them. But just hours later, the man was about to find out the greatest mystery of them all, and according to some religions, he would have to pay for his cruelty to his pitifully damaged son.

Epilogue

My neighbor Tammy met me out front for our evening walk. And she had a brand-new smartphone. She'd been waiting for it to be shipped and was excited to get it.

"Look what I got on it," she said. While Tammy had been telling me about her new phone the night before, I mentioned the free ghost-communicator app that some friends had on theirs. I was under the impression this app was for entertainment purposes only and that it didn't do anything more than generate random words while occasionally showing a fake ghost blip on the little green radar screen. Most ghost hunters are pretty skeptical of these types of things. After all, how do you know it's a real device? For instance, how does it work through a cell phone? There are just too many questions needing answers, and most of the answers can't be proven. It is too unscientific, as my skeptical ghost hunter friend Brian of Massillon

Ghost Hunters Society would say. But then again, psychic abilities are pretty unscientific too. They couldn't fit into the scientific parameters most felt were necessary to be proven. Yet I had proven my own abilities to Brian many times over.

Tammy held out her phone and showed me the radar screen of the ghost communicator. Always up for research at the spur of the moment, I asked her inside my house.

I really didn't expect much.

Tammy told me the communicator app hadn't been showing much of anything at her house, nor had it been reacting while she was out front waiting for me.

We climbed my front steps and came into the front room of my house. I asked her how it worked, and Tammy showed me the screen, which had a fingerprint at the bottom left where you were supposed to place your index finger. I complied and began asking questions.

"Is anybody there?" The random-word generator spelled out "Death." We looked at each other, and Tammy's eyebrows shot up. My husband, Ron, came into the room and joined us. "Can anyone hear me?" I continued. The word on the screen changed to "Penny"—my sister-in-law's name. Then it changed again to "Dane," my brother's name. Then it spelled out "Brooke," my sister's name. Then "book."

"Yes, I just released a book," I said, "and what *about* Penny and Dane?" I thought it was pretty odd that the app would immediately spell out my brother's, his wife's, and my sister's names! The screen flashed "burning," then "kill," then "death" again, then "airplane." My brother and his family did a lot of flying. I was now growing a bit uneasy. What were the odds of a random-word generator app posting my entire family's names out of the blue like this? And mentioning my new book? Pretty slim.

"Who is this?" I asked. And then the screen spelled "James," my deceased son's name! I suddenly felt sick. *How is this possible? I mean, James is a common name, but Dane and Penny? And Brooke? And book?*

"My God, it says James!" I cried out. Now all three of us in the room grew quiet as my mind raced, trying to calculate the odds and discern the possible ramifications.

"James! Is it you? Do you know what happened?" The screen then spelled "car," "kill," "bottle," "innocence," "brain," "backpack," then finally "Ben." *Dear God!* Now I spoke out loud to James, or to whatever random, crazy thing had nailed so many facts in our lives.

"Yes, James was hit by a car on his motorcycle by a drunk driver. He had his new backpack on, the one his best friend Ben gave him just weeks before in California. His skates were in it, and he landed on them, on his back. His brain swelled; that's why he died." It almost felt as though James was giving info he knew would guarantee our recognition. James's old dog, Leia the black Lab, had finally died just weeks before, at age fifteen and a half. Now I asked about this.

"Do you know what happened to Leia?" I waited. The screen flashed the word "Leah," and I lost my breath. James, my husband, and I had called her Leah from the time she was a pup. No one else would know this but us. Now my eyes filled with tears. Then the screen word changed again—"ground." I swallowed back the tears and confirmed this.

"Yes, we buried Leah out back, in the ground." Local laws be damned, we wanted this canine family member near James's other pets who'd had their final resting places in the backyard. I glanced at my neighbor Tammy. She was speechless and had a strange look on her face.

"James, are you okay?" asked my husband. I added a few other questions: Was there a heaven like we thought? Would we see him again? Was anyone with him?

"Linda," flashed the word on the green screen. "Who's Linda?" I said under my breath, wondering about this random name that didn't match anyone in James's or our lives. Tammy whispered, "It's my mom." Her mom had died recently. We stared at each other.

"Honey, are you okay?" I asked again, desperately. "Waves," spelled the app. "I don't understand, what is waves? Are you coming in and out in waves? Is it hard to talk to us?

My husband glanced at me. "I just bought a waves program for recording. James would understand all about that." Since James and his dad had recorded in our music studio for years, James certainly knew the computer programs. Most of the things that had been spelled out made it seem as if James had been watching, as if he was reporting them to us now. If this even *was* him! How was this possible? I'd thought this ghost app was a joke! My husband, who'd switched places with me during our exchange, now said his finger had gone numb, and he had to quit. I could relate to that feeling, that's why I'd had him take over for me. All three of us were uneasy. I couldn't believe this. It was getting late and Tammy and I hadn't had our walk yet. Just in case this was for real, I decided to tell him one last thing. "I love you, James. Even more than ever. Nothing has changed."

"Yes it *has* changed, nothing is the same without you," added my husband sadly. "I'm going now. My finger is asleep." He handed the phone back to Tammy, who was quiet. We were all pretty quiet.

We went on our walk, both deep in thought, not understanding how something that we'd thought was a joke could be so accurate. It felt as though James was there with us for a few minutes. Tammy felt her mom had been there too. We discussed it a little, and later that night, I wrote to my ghost hunter friend Brian to explain what had happened. Brian, ever skeptical, suggested a test, with flashcards, asking to have the app spell out what was on the flashcards. He thought it must be a random coincidence. But I didn't see how it *could* be, considering that of all the words given to us, almost every one was a direct hit.

Disturbed by this, I told a few people, and one even thought it could be something evil, something that had listened to enough of my conversations to know just what was going on. I'd already thought of this and didn't even want to go there. I texted my brother, asking if they had a flight planned anywhere. Luckily, he said no, not until September. If it *was* James, it seemed he knew what had happened, kept up on our lives, and, at least occasionally was here with us. September came and went, and my brother flew to the Virgin Islands and returned safely, leaving me relieved but still wondering.

Could James somehow use this phone app to get messages to us? Maybe it was just a string of random words—just coincidence. There's that word again. Too many coincidences I still don't understand. And I'm afraid to try it again, yet I long to. I still miss James so badly. If James somehow stays aware of us here on earth, he would've watched us bury his old dog out back, he would've known about Ben and the backpack, about what the bottle meant; his killer's drunkenness, which led to James's death; about his brain, and my new books. Just thinking about this is overwhelming. There are no words. May you rest in peace, my sweet boy.

———

While nearing the end of this book, I started thinking about what I've learned, what conclusions I've come to. The more ghost stories I sought out, the more stories seemed to crop up. Friends called and messaged me to tell me they had one to share. I have enough to fill another book, but *this* book is full. The experience of seeking out others' stories to learn more about my own *has* enlightened me; on the one hand, I can see the similarity between theirs and my own experiences. But on the other hand, I understand that just as people are similar yet different, so will they be after their deaths. I realize the saying "as in life, so in death" seems totally accurate, and we are as individual after death as we are in life. I've learned some people retain their quirks, some their sense of humor, others their crotchetiness. Most of all, I've learned we are as interconnected in death as we are in life. And I think I've also learned that I will never be able to stop searching for answers...or for spirits.

To Write the Author

If you wish to contact the author or would like more information about this book, please write to the author in care of Llewellyn Worldwide, and we will forward your request. Both the author and publisher appreciate hearing from you and learning of your enjoyment of this book and how it has helped you. Llewellyn Worldwide cannot guarantee that every letter written to the author can be answered, but all will be forwarded. Please write to:

Debra Robinson
⁄ Llewellyn Worldwide
2143 Wooddale Drive
Woodbury, MN 55125-2989

Please enclose a self-addressed stamped envelope for reply, or $1.00 to cover costs. If outside the USA, enclose an international postal reply coupon.